Samuel French Acting Edition

The Keen Collection
One-Acts by Contemporary Playwrights
Volume 7

Foreign Bodies
by C.A. Johnson

The Rebellious Rhymes of J Nice
by NSangou Njikam

Citizens United
by Kate Cortesi

SAMUELFRENCH.COM   SAMUELFRENCH.CO.UK

Foreign Bodies Copyright © 2020 by C.A. Johnson
The Rebellious Rhymes of J Nice Copyright © 2020 by NSangou Njikam
Citizens United Copyright © 2020 by Kate Cortesi
All Rights Reserved

THE KEEN COLLECTION: VOLUME 7 is fully protected under the copyright laws of the United States of America, the British Commonwealth, including Canada, and all member countries of the Berne Convention for the Protection of Literary and Artistic Works, the Universal Copyright Convention, and/or the World Trade Organization conforming to the Agreement on Trade Related Aspects of Intellectual Property Rights. All rights, including professional and amateur stage productions, recitation, lecturing, public reading, motion picture, radio broadcasting, television and the rights of translation into foreign languages are strictly reserved.

ISBN 978-0-573-70826-8

www.concordtheatricals.com
www.concordtheatricals.co.uk

FOR PRODUCTION ENQUIRIES

UNITED STATES AND CANADA
info@concordtheatricals.com
1-866-979-0447

UNITED KINGDOM AND EUROPE
licensing@concordtheatricals.co.uk
020-7054-7200

Each title is subject to availability from Concord Theatricals, depending upon country of performance. Please be aware that *THE KEEN COLLECTION: VOLUME 7* may not be licensed by Concord Theatricals in your territory. Professional and amateur producers should contact the nearest Concord Theatricals office or licensing partner to verify availability.

CAUTION: Professional and amateur producers are hereby warned that *THE KEEN COLLECTION: VOLUME 7* is subject to a licensing fee. Publication of this play(s) does not imply availability for performance. Both amateurs and professionals considering a production are strongly advised to apply to Concord Theatricals before starting rehearsals, advertising, or booking a theater. A licensing fee must be paid whether the title(s) is presented for charity or gain and whether or not admission is charged. Professional/Stock licensing fees are quoted upon application to Concord Theatricals.

This work is published by Samuel French, an imprint of Concord Theatricals.

No one shall make any changes in this title(s) for the purpose of production. No part of this book may be reproduced, stored in a retrieval system, or transmitted in any form, by any means, now known or yet to be invented, including mechanical, electronic, photocopying, recording, videotaping, or otherwise, without the prior written permission of the publisher. No one shall upload this title(s), or part of this title(s), to any social media websites.

For all enquiries regarding motion picture, television, and other media rights, please contact Concord Theatricals.

MUSIC USE NOTE

Licensees are solely responsible for obtaining formal written permission from copyright owners to use copyrighted music in the performance of this play and are strongly cautioned to do so. If no such permission is obtained by the licensee, then the licensee must use only original music that the licensee owns and controls. Licensees are solely responsible and liable for all music clearances and shall indemnify the copyright owners of the play(s) and their licensing agent, Concord Theatricals, against any costs, expenses, losses and liabilities arising from the use of music by licensees. Please contact the appropriate music licensing authority in your territory for the rights to any incidental music.

IMPORTANT BILLING AND CREDIT REQUIREMENTS

If you have obtained performance rights to this title, please refer to your licensing agreement for important billing and credit requirements.

TABLE OF CONTENTS

About Keen Teens vii
Keen Teens Angels... ix
Foreign Bodies 11
The Rebellious Rhymes of J Nice 41
Citizens United.. 61

ABOUT KEEN TEENS

Founded in 2000, Keen Company is an award-winning Off-Broadway theater producing stories about the decisive moments that change us. Central to Keen Company's mission is to present theatre that patrons can identify with and connect to. The Keen Teens program is the cornerstone of the company's outreach and educational efforts, bringing the company's values to the high school stage by developing new work tailored specifically to teen actors and audiences.

When first creating Keen Teens in 2007, the company found that teachers did not have access to material intended for a high school stage. Educators were left to present either classic plays never designed for teen actors, or material created specifically for school groups that lacked richness or relevance. Through Keen Teens, the company began commissioning original plays and musicals that are as complex and multilayered as the lives of high school students today, penned by accomplished professional playwrights and musical theatre writers.

There are two components to Keen Teens: The first is a free program for New York City-area high school students to work alongside professional writers, directors, and designers to rehearse and premiere these plays Off-Broadway. The second is that the plays then go on to be published and licensed through our partners at Samuel French as *The Keen Collection*.

The Keen Collection is made up of comedies, dramas, and musicals; scripts range from the sincere to the absurd, from the existential to the most intimate. Some deal head-on with topical issues, others simply aim to provide smart, contemporary material. These original pieces have been created by many of the most talented writers working today, including Bekah Brunstetter, Kristoffer Diaz, Madeleine George, C.A. Johnson, Greg Kotis, Mike Lew, James Tyler, Leah Nanako Winkler, and Lauren Yee. This group includes finalists for the Pulitzer, Wendy Wasserstein, and Susan Smith Blackburn Prizes; and winners of the Yale Drama Series Prize, Horton Foote Playwriting Award, and more. Their theatrical work has been produced professionally on and off Broadway, and their writing has reached an international audience on TV shows including *Girls*, *GLOW*, *Mad Men*, *Mozart in the Jungle*, *Nurse Jackie*, *Tales of the City*, and *This Is Us*.

As well as being tailored to the social and emotional world of teens, these plays are also designed to be accessible in educational settings. All scripts run thirty minutes, with simple design elements, large ensembles, and flexible casting requirements. Each play can be presented on its own or in combination with other *Keen Collection* titles on a shared bill.

Keen Teens has made possible the Off-Broadway debut of over three hundred young actors and has led to the publication of over thirty-five new one-act plays and musicals, which are regularly produced not only in the United States, but in countries around the world, from Australia to Singapore.

For more information, please visit www.keencompany.org/teens.

Keen Teens Staff

Robert Ross Parker, *Keen Teens Artistic Producer*
Hope Chavez, *Keen Teens Managing Producer*
Jeremy Stoller, *Director of New Work*

Keen Company

Jonathan Silverstein, *Artistic Director*
Ashley DiGiorgi, *Managing Producer*

KEEN TEENS ANGELS

Keen Teens is generously supported by the Axe-Houghton Foundation, as well as a group of donors affectionately called the Keen Teens Angels:

42nd St. Development Corp., Sandra Abramson, Lindsay Adkins, Joanne Ainsworth, Sarah Alexander, Cathy & Robert Altholz, Billy Amendola, Linda Azarian, Howard Balaban, Marsha Baldinger, Grace Beggins, Amy & Brad Ball, Linda Bartlett, Stephen Belber, Jeffrey Blair & Ivor Clark, Jeffrey & Tina Bolton, Carmen Bowser, Bill & Casey Bradford, Blake & Josh Braford, Karen Bradford, Sara Brandston, Veronique Brossier, Sarah Buterbaugh, Paul Brill, Kathleen Chalfant, Kathy Chazen & Larry Miller, Buena Chilstrom, Maria Cicio, Gary & Ellen Cohen, Katie Cohen, Michael Coratolo, Elizabeth Corradino, Mary Corradino, Rose Courtney, Alexander Coxe, Michael Cristofer, Katherine Crost, Michela Daliana, Lucy & Nathaniel Day, Joseph Deasy, Mia Dillon & Keir Dullea, Marie DiSalvo, Emily Donahoe, Linda D'Onofrio, Kate Donovan, Maralène Downs, Mary Durante, David Ehrich & Chris Shyer, Catherine & Christopher Engel, Gregg Felton, Tony Fingleton, Kenny Finkle, Cathy Frankel, Alice Fricke, Sharon Friedland, Patricia Follert, Jack & Ann Gilpin, Douglas Giombarrese, Barbara Gottlieb, Greg Graham, Timothy Grandia, Roberta Greenberg & Robert Goldy, José Gutierrez, Benjamin Goldberg, Sylvia Golden, Barbara McIntyre Hack, Richard & Edith Hanley, Kathy Harris, Sarah Hauser, Daoud Heidami, Erin Hogan, Victoria Leacock Hoffman, Heidi Hoover, Kimberly Howard, Sally & Robert Huxley, Frank Iryami, Freda Johnson, Kate & David Kies, Stephen Kantor, David & Kate Kies, Jae Kim, Josh Landay, Robert Lane, Judith S. Lidsky, Ginny Louloudes, Kevin & Jana Maher, Marsha Mason, David McMahon, Madeline Marzano-Lesnevich, Monica Lewinsky, Andrew Miltenberg, Cynthia & Bruce Miltenberg, Nancy Morgan, TJ O'Hara, Efren Olivares, Joy Pak, Merrill & Martin Pavane, David & Faith Pedowitz, Michelle Perr, Steven Piscione, Rhonda Pohl & Mark Feldman, David & Katherine Rabinowitz, Rebecca Randall, Angela Reed & Todd Cerveris, Diana Roitman, Nanny Lee Russell, Betsy & Norman Samet, Marta Sanders, Gloria Schalop, Melissa Sexton, Bart Sexton, Susan Shapiro & Bob Piller, Vincent Smith & Alice Silkworth, Neil Simon, Jim Spare, Ron Schwartz, Charles Snipes & Robert Furlong, Olga Staffen, Pat Stockhausen & Mike Emmerman, John Sullivan, Rob Tallia, Jason Tam, Pamela Thomas, Theresa Tolomeo, Ilyse Tretter, Louis Viel, Les Waters, Ben Weintraub, Louly & Bill Williams, Alban Wilson, Marie & Alan Wolpert, Ernest & Judith Wong, Chris Yegen, Alan Zucker

FOREIGN BODIES

C.A. Johnson

FOREIGN BODIES was first produced at Theatre Row in New York City from May 17–19, 2019. The production was directed by Temar Underwood. The cast was as follows:

MALLORY	Victoria Adams
TRISH	Nathalie Jean
ALPHONSE	Jacob Bergman
HAYDEE	Jael Margarita Hoyos
EDDIE	Aidan Doran
CRISSY	Caroline Adams
RAYMOND	Nyles Emile
PENNY	Petra Brusiloff
DEMARCUS	Angel Encarnacion
STACY	Amberrain E. Andrews

CHARACTERS

MALLORY – (twenties) a woman, open ethnicity, a bit volatile, a bit sweet

TRISH – (thirties) a woman of color, smooth, driven

ALPHONSE – (thirties) a man, open ethnicity, a hard worker

HAYDEE – (fifties) a woman of color, a drinker, a watchful eye

EDDIE – (sixties) a man, open ethnicity, a smoker, a kind face

CRISSY – (twenties) a woman, a shit stirrer, but also a mother

RAYMOND – (twenties) a man, open ethnicity, a screwup, but a dedicated card player and a son

STICKY – (forties) a man, open ethnicity, a dedicated card player and a father

PENNY – (teens) a woman, open ethnicity, lost and in love

DEMARCUS – (teens) a man of color, lost and in love or something like it

SETTING

Some place like New Orleans

TIME

Some time like now

AUTHOR'S NOTES

While the categories above use simple binary terms, there are no rules about the use of cis, trans, or non-binary actors in this play. Gender is fluid and should be treated as such in this world.

Sticky and Raymond should be the same ethnicity.

(In darkness, we hear voices.)

MALLORY. Don't.

TRISH. Don't what?

MALLORY. Just don't.

> *(The sound of bed springs shifting, of zippers being zipped, of clothes on body, of a sad sigh. The sound of boots on floor.)*

So that's it, hunh –

TRISH. Mallory, come on –

MALLORY. After all this time you just leave? Just poof into thin air?

TRISH. –

MALLORY. That's great –

TRISH. I'll be back.

MALLORY. When?

TRISH. When time works in our favor.

MALLORY. That's not an answer.

TRISH. It's not like I have another one –

MALLORY. When will I see you? –

TRISH. *(A tiny push.)* When you can, okay?

MALLORY. –

TRISH. *(Softer.)* You'll see me when you can.

> *(The sound of bed springs. A kiss. Then a door opening.)*

You have to promise me you're gonna be okay.

MALLORY. Oh yeah?

TRISH. Yes.

> *(A pause.)*

MALLORY. I'm gonna be okay.

(*Lights shift, and we're inside a bar. Jazz plays on a jukebox,* and the typical weeknight crowd is going through the motions.* **ALPHONSE**, *the bartender with a smile like you won't believe, mixes a drink.* **HAYDEE** *sits at the bar, head buried in her fifth beer of the evening.* **RAYMOND**, **STICKY**, **CRISSY**, *and* **EDDIE** *sit playing a game of Spades. Well,* **EDDIE** *has one foot in a major nap, but he pops awake whenever it's his turn. It's clear that this is a place meant for locals and no one else. In the center of this we find* **MALLORY**. *She's sitting on the bar with her feet on the bar stool. She's two drinks in and half-yelling at* **ALPHONSE**. *He politely listens.*)

MALLORY. She's like this fucking magic person.

Who just took my heart and expanded it so much that it barely fits inside my body,

it's just hanging there all attached and exposed.

I don't even know what to do with it.

And when she looks at me...

...I don't know.

I forget who I am.

I just...become something else.

This whole other thing.

And it's better than being me.

ALPHONSE. –

MALLORY. I wish she'd call more.

Of course.

But all in due time.

ALPHONSE. Mal, can you maybe sit down in that chair?

I just replaced that leather.

---

*A license to produce *Foreign Bodies* does not include a performance license for any third-party or copyrighted music. Licensees should create an original composition or use music in the public domain. For further information, please see Music Use Note on page 3.

MALLORY. Crap. Sorry Alphonse.

ALPHONSE. No need to be sorry. You just gotta contain yourself.
Pain and all.

MALLORY. Pain!
That's what I'm feeling.
I miss her!

HAYDEE. We can see that.

MALLORY. And I don't think she realizes, you know?
How much this is hurting me –

STICKY. *(To the other card players.)* And that's game!

RAYMOND. No way. You cheated.

STICKY. Who cheats in Spades?

RAYMOND. You do.

STICKY. Nunh unh. Me and Eddie won that fair and square. Right Eddie?

  *(**EDDIE** stands.)*

EDDIE. Need a smoke.

  (He goes for the door.)

RAYMOND. Eddie, if you don't come back here and play fair.

EDDIE. *Need* a smoke.

  (And he's gone.)

STICKY. Mallory, come play.
We need a fourth.

MALLORY. No can do.
I'm mid-heartbreak.

CRISSY. We all mid-heartbreak.
Don't mean we can't play cards.

MALLORY. I'm getting therapy from Alphonse.
Can it wait five minutes?

ALPHONSE. No need to wait. Go ahead and play your game.

MALLORY. But you were gonna say something wise, right?
You were gonna fix me?

ALPHONSE. I was actually gonna rinse these glasses.

MALLORY. Oh.

CRISSY. That's cold Alphonse.

> (**ALPHONSE** *shrugs, busying himself with the glassware.*)

STICKY. Come on Mallory. It's you and me versus Ray and Crissy.

RAYMOND. I don't want her to play.

I want a rematch.

STICKY. Just play the damn game, Raymond.

What's the difference between the fifty dollars you lost last night and the fifty you'll lose tonight?

RAYMOND. The difference is winning fair and square.

Which I intend to do.

STICKY. If you say so.

CRISSY. Can we just play this game?

Y'all two can bicker later.

RAYMOND. I just want him to be real.

STICKY. *(Means this.)* And I just want you to pipe down and respect your elders.

Think you can do that?

> (*A small pause.* **RAYMOND** *shrinks a bit. Then* **CRISSY** *deals.*)

CRISSY. Mallory you take Eddie's spot.

> (**MALLORY** *grabs her drink and crosses to the card table.*)

MALLORY. What are the rules again?

RAYMOND. Didn't we already tell her the rules?

CRISSY. It's aight. We'll just tell her again.

Maybe it'll stick this time.

> (*This conversation continues in low tones, with* **CRISSY**, **STICKY**, *and* **RAYMOND** *re-teaching* **MALLORY** *the rules.* **ALPHONSE** *pours a beer and places it in front of* **HAYDEE**

without her having to ask. Then he goes into the back of the bar. As soon as he does, the bar door swings open, and **DEMARCUS** *and* **PENNY** *enter.)*

DEMARCUS. Penny come on now. You know I ain't steppin' out on you, girl.

PENNY. I know you ain't got no business walkin' down St. Peters with Darlene Landry.

DEMARCUS. Who was with Darlene Landry? Me? I never. Not with them busted ass chicken legs on her.

PENNY. Crissy said she seen y'all together more than once. Right Crissy?

CRISSY. *(Not looking up from her cards.)* Leave Crissy out your mouth.

PENNY. You did say it.

CRISSY. Not in front of folks.

*(***DEMARCUS*** grabs ***PENNY*** by the hand, pulling her into him.* ***ALPHONSE*** *appears on the edge of the room.)*

DEMARCUS. Why I need Darlene when I got you, hunh? My sweet Penny girl? –

PENNY. Same reason a snake need an apple even though he got the love of God.

(This gets a laugh from **HAYDEE**.*)*

STICKY. She got you there, youngin'.

DEMARCUS. Shutup, Sticky. Ain't nobody ask you.

STICKY. Look, y'all the one arguing in public. Not me.

PENNY. *(Cutting into this.)* Why you do it, DeMarcus?

DEMARCUS. I ain't do nothin'.

That's what I'm sayin' to you.

PENNY. *Stop lying to me.*

DEMARCUS. –

PENNY. Why?

(The room goes silent. **DEMARCUS** *is embarrassed, but he owes her this much.)*

DEMARCUS. I don't know aight.

I messed up.

I *mess* up.

> (**PENNY** *pulls herself from* **DEMARCUS***'s grip and hurries into the bathroom.*)

Penny wait. Aye Penny come on now.

CRISSY. Leave her be, DeMarcus. Let her think on it.

> (**DEMARCUS** *bangs on the door.*)

DEMARCUS. *Penny!*

PENNY. Leave me alone, DeMarcus. I'm serious.

DEMARCUS. Penny if you don't open this door I swear –

ALPHONSE. *(All authority and calm.)* DEMARCUS!

> *(A pause rings around the room. Then* **DEMARCUS** *backs away from the door. He moves toward the exit, but stops when he sees* **MALLORY**.*)*

DEMARCUS. Hey, Mal.

MALLORY. Hey, DeMarcus.

DEMARCUS. Your girl call today?

MALLORY. Not yet.

DEMARCUS. Well…keep your head up.

> *(He exits.)*

CRISSY. *(To* **MALLORY**.*)* See that.

That's what worries me about you.

MALLORY. What?

CRISSY. The one person who understands what's going through your head ain't nothing but a backwards child.

MALLORY. DeMarcus is not backwards.

STICKY. Course he is.

Both of them are.

MALLORY. They're just in love.

And love is hard –

HAYDEE. *(Cutting in from her perch.)* Love ain't one bit of hard actually.

It's soft.

Like snow.

You oughta know that, child.

Much as you been carryin' on.

> *(**MALLORY** just looks at **HAYDEE**. The others avert their eyes. A breath. Then **CRISSY** plays her next hand, breaking the tension.)*
>
> *(**EDDIE** enters. He sees that **MALLORY** has taken his spot and hops onto a stool. **ALPHONSE** pours him a beer and places it in front of him.)*
>
> *(Lights out. In darkness, we hear voices and the steady sound of live music from an adjacent room. It gets louder over the next.*)*

MALLORY. Tell me again about the stars.

TRISH. I don't remember saying nothin' about the stars.

MALLORY. You did.

In my dream you told me about how the stars and the planets are aligned.

How the whole solar system is moving and changing but it's really just finding new formations.

And each formation says something about us.

About who we are.

TRISH. That don't sound like me.

MALLORY. But it was you.

You spoke to me.

TRISH. I spoke to you?

MALLORY. Yes.

You floated towards me on a paddle boat.

---

*A license to produce *Foreign Bodies* does not include a performance license for any third-party or copyrighted music. Licensees should create an original composition or use music in the public domain. For further information, please see Music Use Note on page 3.

We just sat there for hours, soaking in the night sky.

> *(A pause.)*

TRISH. Sometimes you sound crazy, you know?

Like...you sound off?

MALLORY. –

TRISH. And you get this look.

A real far off look.

MALLORY. Okay so you don't want to talk about the stars –

TRISH. You *okay* right, Mal?

You okay with all this.

With you and me?

MALLORY. Course I'm okay, stupid.

> *(A pause. The sound of covers shifting, of bodies intertwining.)*

Tell me about music then.

Tell me about your horn.

TRISH. What about my horn?

MALLORY. Anything. Everything.

Talk to me like it's a Monday night at One-Eyed Pats and I'm the prettiest girl in the room.

TRISH. We don't talk at Pats.

MALLORY. Then just play for me, Trish.

Play me your best song.

And I promise I'll listen.

> *(A breath. Then the sound of a trumpet floats toward us, clear and bright.*)*
>
> *(Lights shift, and we're back inside the bar. **EDDIE** and **HAYDEE** sit in chairs facing the audience. **HAYDEE** holds a glass of beer and drinks. **ALPHONSE** is behind the bar, stocking,*

---

*A license to produce *Foreign Bodies* does not include a performance license for any third-party or copyrighted music. Licensees should create an original composition or use music in the public domain. For further information, please see Music Use Note on page 3.

cleaning, and generally being the best damn bartender there ever was.)

EDDIE. Haydee been here fifty years.
I been here twenty-three.

HAYDEE. Twenty-four you been here.
God's truth.

EDDIE. Twenty-four then.
And we seen it all.
They all come in with their eyes on whatever is botherin' 'em.
And they whine and cry about it.
They sing and dance and play cards and fuck until one day it hits 'em.

HAYDEE. Best to let go.

EDDIE. Best to live in the now.

HAYDEE. All that is over now.

EDDIE. All that *was* is over now.

*(He looks at **HAYDEE**. Smiles.)*

HAYDEE. Then they got a choice.
The big choice.

EDDIE. Sure do.

HAYDEE. Stay or go.

EDDIE. Live a lil bit more.

HAYDEE. Or call it quits.

EDDIE. And Haydee and me.
We choose to stay.
We choose to sip and laugh.
For as long as we allowed.
Ain't that right, Alphonse?

ALPHONSE. I really should work.

EDDIE. Alphonse chose too.
Nobody know how long ago.

HAYDEE. He just here.
He just be.

EDDIE. For how long you think, Al?

ALPHONSE. Long as it take.

> *(A pause. **EDDIE** takes **HAYDEE**'s hand and kisses it. She blushes despite herself and sips her beer. Then **EDDIE** pats his shirt pocket.)*

EDDIE. Need a smoke.

> *(Lights shift, and we're still in the bar. **EDDIE** and **HAYDEE** are gone. **CRISSY** and **RAYMOND** are playing a game of gin rummy. **ALPHONSE** is sitting on a stool, sipping a beer.)*

CRISSY. You gotta stop letting Sticky get under your skin.

RAYMOND. He ain't under my skin.

CRISSY. He say jump, you jump too damn high, and both of y'all cry about it.

> *(They play.)*

RAYMOND. I just don't understand why I'm here.

CRISSY. Give it time.

RAYMOND. I don't have time.

CRISSY. Sure you do.

You got all the time in the world if you want it.

> *(They play.)*

RAYMOND. He used to be different.

Sticky.

He used to smile. All the time.

And he used to carry candies.

Little butterscotches and peppermints in his purse like he was an old, old man.

I would tug and tug on his hands for hours, waiting for him to look down at me and place a candy in my palm.

> *(They play.)*

Does he remember any of that?

> *(**CRISSY** looks up from the game and at **RAYMOND**. A beat. Then **CRISSY** sits back.)*

ALPHONSE. Hey Alphonse, won't you play us something?

> *(He goes behind the bar and turns on a slow, moving jazz tune. Something where a trombone just rolls and rolls along.* **CRISSY** keeps her eyes on **RAYMOND**, who's turned toward the sound.)*

CRISSY. When I first got here, Sticky was a strung-out dope fiend stealing everybody's money and hanging in abandoned houses to make due.

He would come in this bar, eyes empty, soul dark.

And he'd ask me and Alphonse for respite.

I was waiting tables then. If you can believe it.

So we'd pour him a cup, fix him up some red beans and rice, talk to him civil.

Course by the time Sticky was gone, we was twenty dollars short and pissed about it.

We ain't pick a fight though.

We ain't cut him off.

We ain't curse him.

We just keep giving.

'Til one day it seem he forget all them things.

He forget he hurt.

He heal.

He started up our lil card-playin' club.

He started buyin' records for the player. Like this one.

He committed to us. To something good.

Something he can hold in his hands without it killing him.

Can you understand that? –

RAYMOND. But does he remember me?

CRISSY. –

---

*A license to produce *Foreign Bodies* does not include a performance license for any third-party or copyrighted music. Licensees should create an original composition or use music in the public domain. For further information, please see Music Use Note on page 3.

RAYMOND. He's my dad, Crissy –

CRISSY. *Was.*

He was your daddy.

Now he something new.

    (A pause.)

RAYMOND. How long have you been here?

CRISSY. Long enough.

RAYMOND. You ever plan on leaving?

CRISSY. We all plan on leaving someday, Raymond.

But if we still sittin' here sippin' ale, there's gotta be a reason.

RAYMOND. You sayin' Sticky's got unfinished business?

CRISSY. I'm sayin' I just wanna play cards.

Can you just play cards with me?

    *(**RAYMOND** keeps his eyes on **CRISSY** for a beat, then he plays his hand. As **CRISSY** preps her next play, **RAYMOND** looks skyward.)*

RAYMOND. Hey Alphonse, can you turn that up?

    *(**ALPHONSE** does, and trombone rings around the room.* It goes around and around and around, and **RAYMOND** goes with it.)*

ALPHONSE. I always loved this one.

    (Lights shift. In darkness, we hear voices. One voice calls to the other through a closed door.)

MALLORY. Okay so I get a little possessive.

I know that.

But can you blame me?

Who knows when I'm gonna see you.

With the amount you're gone. With all the late night sessions and the band meetings.

---

*A license to produce *Foreign Bodies* does not include a performance license for any third-party or copyrighted music. Licensees should create an original composition or use music in the public domain. For further information, please see Music Use Note on page 3.

TRISH. It's the twenty-first century, Mal.
If you miss me you can just call me.
Text me.
Whatever.

MALLORY. I know that.

TRISH. And if you want to see me, you can tag along to shows.

MALLORY. But your bandmates hate me.

TRISH. That's all in your head.
How many times do I have to say that.

MALLORY. It's not in my head.

TRISH. It is. And it's gotta stop.
You have to stop.

(A small pause. A door opens.)

MALLORY. I just want to feel you, Trish.
Even when you're two counties away I want to be able to reach out my hands and just touch you.
So I know you're mine.

(A pause.)

TRISH. I ever tell you about the time I almost popped my lower lip.
It's dangerous, horn playing.
All those hours, lips pressed to metal, all that strain.
I was in this contest with Willie Banks, trying to blow and blow on this high C.
And I got there. Willie too. But then he wanted to double down, and I could feel it in my cheeks.
I needed to stop.
But I didn't.
I picked up my horn and blew and blew.
Time I was done my whole face was numb.
Doctor said I nearly tore the lip muscle.
Could've ended my career if it was bad enough.

MALLORY. Why are you telling me this?

TRISH. If you chase the note too hard, you might not ever reach it.

Just be with me, Mal.

Just be good with being with me.

> *(Lights shift.)*
>
> *(We see two bathroom stalls, and beneath their closed doors, the feet of two women. One of them is crying. After a pause, the other leans toward the partition.)*

MALLORY. Hey.

PENNY. –

MALLORY. Hey, Penny?

PENNY. –

MALLORY. Could you pass some tissue?

> *(**PENNY** passes a wad of tissue under the stall.)*

You okay?

PENNY. I'm fine.

MALLORY. You don't sound fine.

…You sure you don't want to come out into the bar.

Talk to somebody?

PENNY. Somebody like who? You?

MALLORY. Sure.

If you wanted to –

PENNY. I got no interest in talking to you.

> *(A pause.)*

MALLORY. DeMarcus hasn't come back yet.

PENNY. –

MALLORY. In case you were wondering –

PENNY. He's probably out on the street.

Searching.

…But they say we shouldn't wander.

They say it's better to find your people.

Find a home in this place.

Or leave it behind.

MALLORY. Who's they?
PENNY. *They*, Mallory.
>(*A pause.*)

MALLORY. What are you talking about?
>(**PENNY** *takes a deep breath.*)

PENNY. You talk to your girl today, Mal?
MALLORY. No not yet.
But I left her a message.
PENNY. Oh yeah.
When?
MALLORY. Earlier.
PENNY. When exactly, Mallory?
Here in the bar or back at your place?
Where was you standin'?
What was you holdin' in your hand?
MALLORY. I don't understand what you're asking me.
PENNY. She ain't callin', Mallory.
…She ain't never callin'.
>(*Lights shift.*)
>(*In darkness, we hear voices.*)

MALLORY. We should get married.
TRISH. What?
MALLORY. We should get married –
TRISH. –
MALLORY. Nothing big.
We could just go to the courthouse, sign some papers, and then throw a big picnic in your grandma's backyard.
Just good food and conversation and the people we love.
TRISH. Is this like a legitimate proposal or –
MALLORY. And we can hire a DJ…or your band! We could totally hire your band!
TRISH. Mallory what is going on –
MALLORY. It could be twenties-themed.

Everybody in flapper dresses with their hair pinned.

You in a suit looking dapper.

Me in off-white.

Don't want to lie to the masses. You know what I mean –

TRISH. *Mallory.*

> (**MALLORY** *stops. The sound of bed springs shifting beneath weight.*)

MALLORY. So you don't want to marry me?

TRISH. Today? No.

Tomorrow? Definitely not.

A year or two from now? Maybe. Definite, maybe.

MALLORY. Well that's great –

TRISH. Look are you good, Mal?

Are you like…good?

MALLORY. Why do you always ask me that?

TRISH. Because you never properly answer the question.

MALLORY. According to you –

TRISH. And because I care about the answer, Mal.

I care about you.

Can't you see that?

MALLORY. But you won't marry me?

> (*A pause.*)

TRISH. I need to take a shower.

> (*The sound of feet on floor. Then of a shower starting up. A few beats pass, and then* **MALLORY** *yields.*)

MALLORY. Okay maybe marriage is a stretch.

> (*A pause. Then music starts up in the bathroom.**)

Trish?

---

*A license to produce *Foreign Bodies* does not include a performance license for any third-party or copyrighted music. Licensees should create an original composition or use music in the public domain. For further information, please see Music Use Note on page 3.

(Lights shift.)

(We're back in the bar. **CRISSY**, **EDDIE**, **STICKY**, *and* **RAYMOND** *play cards.* **MALLORY** *sits on a stool, nursing a beer.* **HAYDEE** *sits on her stool without a drink.* **ALPHONSE** *is nowhere to be seen.)*

(To no one in particular.) I've made a decision!

CRISSY. Oh good.

STICKY. 'Bout time.

MALLORY. If Raymond can stop complaining every other day about losing at Spades, then I can stop yammering on about Trish.

CRISSY. Damn straight!

STICKY. 'Bout time.

HAYDEE. *(Completely serious.)* Who the hell is Trish?

MALLORY. My girl.
Leather vest, plays a horn?
My one and only.

HAYDEE. Never heard of her.

MALLORY. I talk about her every night.
I sit here and I tell you and Alphonse and everybody here about her.
About all those nights wrapped in sheets.
About her music.

HAYDEE. Sorry, honey.
But I got no memory of that.
    (A pause.)

MALLORY. Then I'll tell you again.
We met at this concert at Wicked Willy's. I was going apeshit on a plate of barbecue and we locked eyes...
Then she smiled at me.
I hadn't been smiled at in a long time.
By anyone.
She smiled at me. she came over, and she said...
What did she say...

(She thinks about it.)

MALLORY. Shit. What did she say?

HAYDEE. Better keep your story child.
Won't matter for much longer.

> *(And with that, **HAYDEE** stands up. She crosses to **EDDIE** and gives him a kiss on the top of his head.)*

Better tell 'em all, Eddie.

> *(She exits the bar without looking back.)*

MALLORY. Why can't I remember what she said?

EDDIE. Apologies, Mallory.
I'm too tired to hold your hand right now.
Got an announcement to make.

CRISSY. An announcement?

STICKY. What sort of announcement?

EDDIE. Alphonse has left the building.

> *(A pause.)*

CRISSY. *What?*

EDDIE. He passed on in the middle of his day shift.
Only Haydee was here to see it.
She said he went easy.

> *(They let that hang. They all take it in.)*

CRISSY. I think we oughta head home.
Close up for the night out of respect.

STICKY. Seconded.

EDDIE. Then it's settled. We go home.

> *(They all stand, stacking the cards and heading for the doors. **MALLORY** and **RAYMOND** hesitate.)*

MALLORY. Wait what are we doing?

STICKY. Packing up.

MALLORY. But why?
What happened to Alphonse?

STICKY. We should pack it up I said.

RAYMOND. I think you should just answer her question, Sticky.

She asked politely.

Didn't she?

> *(A pause.* **CRISSY** *and* **EDDIE** *look to* **STICKY**, *who gestures them away. They exit.* **STICKY** *looks at* **RAYMOND** *for a pause.)*

STICKY. Ask me that again.

MALLORY. Where did Alphonse go exactly?

STICKY. On.

MALLORY. On to what?

STICKY. *(To* **RAYMOND**.*)* I can't help her.

You have to help her.

RAYMOND. Why me? Why not you? –

STICKY. *Snap out of it, Raymond.*

> *(A pause. Then* **STICKY** *crosses to* **RAYMOND** *and puts a hand on his chest.)*

Be sure.

You have to be sure.

RAYMOND. What exactly am I being sure of?

STICKY. Everything.

And nothing.

Then it all just goes away.

RAYMOND. –

STICKY. You get what I'm saying?

RAYMOND. You remember me, don't you?

> *(***STICKY** *puts a hand on* **RAYMOND***'s shoulder and squeezes. There is some version of recognition in this gesture.)*

Cards tomorrow, yeah?

> *(***STICKY** *exits.* **RAYMOND** *takes that in.)*

MALLORY. Was all of that supposed to mean something to me?

RAYMOND. *(A release.)* How did you get here, Mallory?

MALLORY. I walked here.

RAYMOND. No not to this bar. To this street. To this town.

MALLORY. I walked here.

RAYMOND. Think, Mallory. Just slow your brain down and remember.

> (*A pause.* **MALLORY** *thinks and doesn't like what she finds.*)

MALLORY. I don't understand what you're asking me.

RAYMOND. I floated here.

I was in a canal off Airline Highway.

My throat was clogged with blood and dirt, but I floated here all on my own.

Right into my bed.

And when I woke up I walked here.

I came right through those doors and I was home.

MALLORY. ...Raymond, you're not making any sense –

RAYMOND. I got into a fight with my mom one night.

I told her to fuck off, then I hopped in my car, and I drove.

I was wasted, but I got behind the wheel anyway, and eventually...I crashed into a telephone pole.

My body was flung from the car, over the railing, and into a canal.

Impact was bad, but it was the water that did me in.

In too much pain to pick up my own head.

MALLORY. –

RAYMOND. I drowned, Mallory.

MALLORY. –

RAYMOND. Now.

What happened to you?

> (**MALLORY** *is quiet for many moments. Then...*)

MALLORY. I don't know.

> *(The bathroom door opens, and* **PENNY** *enters.* **MALLORY** *and* **RAYMOND** *turn to her.)*

RAYMOND. Penny.
You've been in that bathroom for days.

PENNY. I have?

RAYMOND. Yeah.

PENNY. Where's DeMarcus?
I need him.

RAYMOND. Nobody's seen him.
Maybe he moved on.

PENNY. Without me?

> *(***RAYMOND** *shrugs.)*

RAYMOND. They say sometimes it happens that way.
Say sometimes it's not about coming together.
It's about breaking apart.

> *(A small pause.)*

You should know Alphonse is gone.
Bar's done for the night.

> *(With that,* **RAYMOND** *exits.* **PENNY** *looks at the door where he was, and then she looks at* **MALLORY**.*)*

PENNY. You all right?

> *(Lights shift.)*

> *(We are in a bedroom.* **TRISH** *sits on one edge of the bed.* **MALLORY** *sits on the opposite edge. They aren't looking at one another.)*

MALLORY. I don't understand.

TRISH. It's a tour, Mal.
All the major cities and then we'll do an international leg.
It's a big deal.

MALLORY. But you'll be gone for seven months.

TRISH. Yes, I will.

> *(A pause.)*

TRISH. At least say you're excited for me.

MALLORY. I'm excited for you.

TRISH. Can you maybe sound like you mean it?

MALLORY. I don't think so.

>   (**TRISH** *looks at* **MALLORY**, *but* **MALLORY** *won't look back at her.*)

TRISH. I have to pack.
 We leave in the morning.

MALLORY. –

TRISH. Mallory? –

MALLORY. Can you believe I asked you to marry me?
 I'm such an idiot.
 We barely know each other.

TRISH. Sure we do.

MALLORY. Really? Tell me one real thing you know about me?

TRISH. I know you're a Taurus.
 And I know we talk to each other in your dreams, remember?
 We rap about the stars.

MALLORY. I don't know shit about the stars.

TRISH. You know everything about the stars, Mal.
 Everything.

>   (*A pause.*)

 Don't make me go like this.

>   (*She reaches for* **MALLORY**, *but* **MALLORY** *evades the touch.*)

MALLORY. Don't.

TRISH. Don't what?

MALLORY. Just don't.

>   (**TRISH** *stands. She gets dressed for a pause.*)

 So that's it, hunh –

TRISH. Mallory, come on –

MALLORY. After all this time you just leave?

Just poof into thin air?

TRISH. –

MALLORY. That's great –

TRISH. I'll come back.

MALLORY. When?

TRISH. When time works in our favor.

MALLORY. That's not an answer.

TRISH. It's not like I have another one –

MALLORY. When will I see you? –

TRISH. *(A tiny push.)* When you can, okay?

MALLORY. –

TRISH. *(Softer.)* You'll see me when you can.

> *(She crosses to **MALLORY**. A kiss.)*

You have to promise me you're gonna be okay.

MALLORY. Oh yeah?

TRISH. Yes.

> *(A pause.)*

MALLORY. I'm gonna be okay.

> **(TRISH** *exits.* **MALLORY** *sits there for many moments. Then she closes her eyes.)*
>
> *(Lights shift. We're in the bar.* **MALLORY** *sits with* **DEMARCUS**. **HAYDEE** *is behind the bar, cleaning.)*

I thought you were gone.

Raymond said you were gone.

DEMARCUS. I was waiting for you.

MALLORY. But you two are tied.

You're always together.

DEMARCUS. We came here together, yeah.

But that's our old story.

I'm writing a new one now.

MALLORY. Why is everybody talking in riddles all of a sudden? Am I supposed to know what you're all talking about?

DEMARCUS. How did you get here, Mallory?

MALLORY. I walked.

DEMARCUS. No, *how* did you get here?

> (*A pause. Then the sound of a trumpet, clear and bright.*)

MALLORY. A song I think.

DEMARCUS. Oh yeah?

MALLORY. I was humming a tune.
Her tune.
Sitting on my bathroom floor.
There were pills?
I was really sad.

DEMARCUS. What were you sad about?

MALLORY. I grab onto everything bad in the world sometimes.
All at once.
And it overwhelms me.

> (**DEMARCUS** *nods.*)

I scared her off.
And then I stopped taking my meds. I should always take my meds.
'Cause when I don't...I break promises.

> (*A small pause.*)

Pretty messed up that this looks like home, right?

DEMARCUS. Pretty much.

MALLORY. It even smells like home but...

> (*She can't quite find the words.* **DEMARCUS** *takes her hand.*)

DEMARCUS. Look up, Mallory.

> (**MALLORY** *looks at him, and then, together, they look up. They see the stars.*)

That right there...that's Ursa Major. And if you follow the line from that bottom right star to the top right one and keep going up...that's the North Star.

MALLORY. Okay.

Am I supposed to follow that?

DEMARCUS. Fuck if I know. I'm just tellin' you what I see, sis.

MALLORY. –

DEMARCUS. What do you see?

MALLORY. I don't know.

DEMARCUS. Look hard.

> (**MALLORY** *does. As she does this, the bar door opens and* **EDDIE** *enters, followed by* **PENNY**, **CRISSY**, **STICKY**, *and* **RAYMOND**. *They all look up.*)

MALLORY. Well I'll be.

HAYDEE. Welcome home, child.

> (*The trumpet swells. Maybe a trombone joins in.* They all inhale.*)
>
> (*Lights.*)

End of Play

---

*A license to produce *Foreign Bodies* does not include a performance license for any third-party or copyrighted music. Licensees should create an original composition or use music in the public domain. For further information, please see Music Use Note on page 3.

THE REBELLIOUS RHYMES OF J NICE

NSangou Njikam

THE REBELLIOUS RHYMES OF J NICE was first produced at Theatre Row in New York City from May 17–19, 2019. The production was directed by Dennis A. Allen III. The cast was as follows:

J NICE	Leanora Octavia Tapper
ROK	Amberrain E. Andrews
EVIDENCE	Brianna Dodd
CHERISH	Brooke Lyn Sicignano
MAKEDA	A'dreana Williams
RAE	Jaylene Gonzalez
ALANA	Deena Langhorn
LEAN	Holliday Senquiz

CHARACTERS

THE REBELS

J NICE – (Emcee) African American female
ROK – African American female
EVIDENCE – African American female
CHERISH – African American or Latina female

MAKEDA'S CREW

MAKEDA – (Emcee) African American female
RAE – African American or Latina female
ALANA – African American or Latina female

THE REFEREE

LEAN – African American or Latina female

SETTING

A South Bronx high school lobby

AUTHOR'S NOTES

All characters are high school age and either Black or Latinx. The rhymes are done a cappella, with the emcees sounding more like Ultimate Rap League rappers/spoken-word poets rather than emcees who rhyme over a beat. The idea is to use rhymes as punchlines.

For Jaela

(Pushing through the darkness of the stage is the voice of Jennice Livingston, known from this point by her emcee name, **J NICE**.*)*

J NICE. To the Creator of all things…to the Ancestors who spit rhymes before me…I come to you this day thanking you for breath, life, and the power to use the Spoken Word. Today, I have to battle for the title. For the championship. I know it's You that make sure my bars stay lit, so give me the fire that will turn her rhymes to dust. No matter what challenge she presents, may I always overcome. This is my time…J Nice time. Rebels battle 'til we've won. In the name of the Creator and all my Ancestors…Ase.

(Lights rise on **J NICE**, *center stage, holding a cup of water. Next to her is her friend* **ROK**.*)*

ROK. Ase. What's "Ase" mean?

J NICE. Our Ancestors said Ase to make things come into existence. It's a word of Power.

ROK. Ase. I like that. And the water?

*(***J NICE*** pours a few drops on the ground, then drinks.)*

J NICE. Now I'm ready.

ROK. Do all emcees do this?

J NICE. I dunno. The Rebels do it.

ROK. And that's why you win so many battles?

J NICE. It's part of it. What time is it?

ROK. 3:11. You nervous?

J NICE. Why would I be nervous?

ROK. Jennice, you're about to battle Makeda Baker…Queen of the Cypher in the South Bronx. I'm worried and I ain't even rhyming.

J NICE. I don't worry. I win. Win and worry can't exist in the same space. I only focus on winning.

ROK. Right. I mean, Ase.

J NICE. I been training for this all year, you know. This is my dream Rok. Can you imagine what it would mean to defeat Makeda Baker? To become the new Champion of the BX? This is major shit.

ROK. The Rebels would take the game over. We could be on Ultimate Rap League. I could get my bars all the way up, and take on Rae or Alana in a public battle. Then we could drop bars on all of New York. All of the country! Just crazy bars on these bitches ALL DAY! Smacking emcees on Pay-Per-View What!

J NICE. Not so fast. You gotta get your rhymes up. You just became a Rebel. There's a lot of steps before we let you smack down anything.

ROK. Ase.

J NICE. And don't say "Ase" too much. Don't be too casual with God's power. Respect it.

ROK. As– I mean aight.

J NICE. Here come the rest of the Rebels.

*(Enter **CHERISH** and **EVIDENCE**.)*

What up Rebels?

CHERISH. Another day, another ass whupping from the rhymes of J Nice.

J NICE. You already know.

EVIDENCE. What up Newbie Sue?

ROK. What?

EVIDENCE. You new. You ain't proven you really a Rebel, yet.

ROK. I'm down. I been here with J Nice helping her get ready. Been working on bars and shit. Where you be? Where was y'all?

EVIDENCE. Don't worry about that, Newbie Sue. We handled our mission.

J NICE. Whatchu got?

CHERISH. Apparently Makeda's boyfriend Xavier just dropped her last night. Through Snapchat.

ROK. Damn that's...

J NICE. Perfect. Anything else?

EVIDENCE. I heard she got a D on the last History test. The whole test was on Black History. How the hell you Black and not gonna know Black History? Dumb ass.

ROK. Wait, you went and got dirt on Makeda?

EVIDENCE. In case you weren't clear, that's how these battles go. Everybody gets dirt on the opponent before the battle. Almost nothing is off limits. Almost...nothing.

ROK. Like?

CHERISH. Depends on the emcee. But certain shit, like real important or personal shit...we don't touch that. But you gotta be ready for anything in the Cypher.

ROK. How do you find the dirt?

EVIDENCE. Yo, too many questions Newbie Sue. You just got here.

J NICE. Yo Evidence, chill.

EVIDENCE. J, I don't like all the questions. That's mad suspect.

CHERISH. Ev, she's new.

EVIDENCE. Then she should be quiet and observe. Listen before you speak.

J NICE. Cherish, Evidence...do me a favor and head to the Cypher.

EVIDENCE. And Newbie Sue?

J NICE. Gimme a minute with her.

>   (**EVIDENCE** gestures to **ROK** as if to say, "I'm watching you." **EVIDENCE** and **CHERISH** leave.)

Don't sweat it Rok. You wouldn't be here if we ain't want you here.

ROK. Just trying to learn the game.

J NICE. I know, but maybe the best way to learn is to listen. If you need to know, we'll tell you.

ROK. I hear you. I just wanna be like…like the shit. I wanna know all the things. And learning how y'all get dirt on your opponents is like a thing I needed to know.

J NICE. That's a secret weapon. But there's nuances to it. You gotta know when you might've gone too far. You remember that story I shared with you?

ROK. About what happened to that girl. How she got hurt by some boys, like hurt really bad. Was gone from her friends for weeks, living in nothing but darkness, but when she returned she was like a new human. Powerful. She could use her words like Wonder Woman's armbands. She could take down any rapper, woman or man. That one?

J NICE. That girl was me.

ROK. Wait for real?

J NICE. Yep. That's a special story. Nothing to be retelling. I shared it with you so you could understand this is beyond just being known to spit rhymes. I don't do this to impress people. I need to do this. For myself.

(**ROK** *looks shocked.*)

What?

ROK. I just didn't know. Thought you were telling a fictional story. Damn J Nice…this changes the whole thing for me.

J NICE. Now you know. I told you that story because I trust you in my crew. You a Rebel. We fight until we win.

ROK. Ase.

J NICE. Ready to go?

ROK. Uh…yeah. Yeah. You ready?

J NICE. J Nice was born ready. Let's get that championship.

(*A beat drops as* **CHERISH** *and* **EVIDENCE** *re-enter.**
MAKEDA *enters with her* **CREW**, *consisting of*

---

*A license to produce *The Rebellious Rhymes of J Nice* does not include a performance license for any third-party or copyrighted music. Licensees should create an original composition or use music in the public domain. For further information, please see Music Use Note on page 3.

ALANA *and* **RAE**. *The referee for the battle,* **LEAN**, *enters from upstage as the two* **CREWS** *face each other in an emcee standoff.*)

LEAN. Hear ye, hear ye. We are gathered to this Cypher this fine afternoon for the battle we have been waiting for. We been talking about it all year, and now it is finally here. Today, we will witness a battle for the Championship of the South Bronx. To my right, the challenger. She's been slaying rappers all year long and is now the number one contender for the title. Give it up for the leader of the Rebels…J Niiiiiiiiice!

(*The* **REBELS** *cheer.*)

And to my left, the champion. Really needing no introduction. She has defended her title a total of ten times this year alone. Give it up for the pride and joy of the South Bronx…the Queen of the Emcees…Makedaaaaaaa Baaaaaker!

(**MAKEDA'S CREW** *goes crazy.*)

I am the judge and referee, Lean. And though I may have a natural gangsta lean I am not partial to any side. I don't care who wins as long as the flows is tight. That being said, here are the rules. I mean, there aren't really any rules but just don't take shit too far. And remember, don't take no of this shit personal.

ALL. It's just rhyming.

LEAN. Will the emcees step forward.

(**MAKEDA** *and* **J NICE** *step to center.* **LEAN** *pulls out a coin.*)

Makeda, you're the champ. Heads or tails?

MAKEDA. Don't matter either way. Let her choose.

J NICE. Sure you want that?

MAKEDA. J Nice you got a few bars, but not enough to take the crown. So you pick your destruction. Either way, it's coming.

J NICE. Heads.

(LEAN flips the coin. It lands.)

LEAN. It's tails. J Nice. You're up first.

(The EMCEES retreat to their crews.)

MAKEDA. What y'all think?

ALANA. Light work, son.

RAE. Yeah but she be on all that Woke shit. She's like real Wakandan with hers.

ALANA. That's not even a real country.

RAE. Still!

MAKEDA. I don't care.

RAE. You want the bomb?

MAKEDA. Naw, save that info. I may not even need it. She won't last two rounds.

(Lights shift to J NICE and the REBELS.)

CHERISH. You got this J Nice. She don't expect you to hang on.

EVIDENCE. Go hard in the paint. Make sure to mix Woke with Rachet. Keep her on her toes.

ROK. Right and…uh…Ase!

EVIDENCE. What?

ROK. I dunno. Just helping.

EVIDENCE. Way too thirsty, son.

J NICE. I got it. This is for the title.

(The EMCEES take their positions.)

Aight…check me out y'all. This right here been a long time coming/a lot of people talking but not saying nothing/their talk is just stuffing/Rappers like you is eggs, bacon and cheese/McMuffin/Consider this the Underground Railroad/I'm Harriet Tubman/you ain't nothing but a protest/I'm the whole revolution/this chick think she a problem but/clearly I'm the solution/opened her mouth and all I see is pollution/my flows make you talk crooked/she need help/elocution/my flows are like the Law/I stay setting precedents/your shit is older than Moses/I'm the New Testament/your reign is now over/I'm raining Threes like Steph Curry/ You assed out like the donkey in Shrek/somebody call up Eddie Murphy!

(The **REBELS** *cheer.* **MAKEDA** *steps forward.)*

MAKEDA. That was cute. Aight...you gonna take the crown?/ naw There must be some confusion/only way you taking my shit is if you down with Russian collusion/my flows is straight butter/your shit be wobbling like it's jelly/ stop tryna mess with the grownups/you a minor, dog/R Kelly/yeah I said it/you a minor/I'm a major like a college degree/speaking of Eddie Murphy, let's call you Dr. DooLittle/you can't rap with my pedigree/See I stay blazing like fire/you barely just a spark/think she came up short on ideas/your rhymes look like Kevin Hart/ your bars, they can't stand up/I'm not a protest, baby I'm the police/Hands Up/better get used to failing/ you will never touch my success/my rhymes make the people say "Ho"/your ass is just a Ho-tep.

*(***MAKEDA'S CREW** *goes crazy.)*

LEAN. Dayum! This is a battle! Round One definitely goes to Makedaaaaaaaaaa! Let's pause for the cause before we go to Round Two.

(The **EMCEES** *retreat to their crews.)*

ROK. You good, Jennice?

J NICE. Yeah I'm good. Just the first round.

EVIDENCE. Don't sweat it, but you gotta come back hard. I told you she'll be prepared for the Woke lines.

J NICE. I hear you, Ev. I'll go harder in Round Two.

CHERISH. You got to. If you take her to the third round you can win this.

J NICE. I got this. Rebels fight 'til we win.

LEAN. And we are back for Round Two. Aight, J Nice. Makeda turned up a bit. You gotta come back strong. Lucky for you, Makeda starts this round off. Y'all ready?

(The **EMCEES** *nod.)*

LEAN. Let's get it on!

MAKEDA. See...that last verse you spit?/that's The best you got/J Nice must think she's Hamilton/she only got one shot/Me, I'm explosive and my clip stay loaded/I got her rhymes like Disney on Ice/her shit stay Frozen/naw see, I'm a whole pack of smokes/you just a Loosey/I'm a give you cheap shots like H&M/then switch it up and go straight Gucci/I'm Bruce Lee/I accept challenges all day, whenever/even when I retire I'll still beat your ass/call me Mayweather/am I affected by the things you say?/Hardly, B/when I'm done you'll delete your Instagram and Twitter/Cardi B/when I A-ttack, you gonna cover your head like a snapback/these is real facts/I'll clap back on videos like Snapchat/Rappers honor my name/they look at you in disgrace/where your Woke rhymes at now, kid/I left your ass in the Sunken Place.

*(***MAKEDA'S CREW**, *once again, goes crazy.)*

LEAN. Makeda got more bars than prison. Aight J Nice. Whatchu got?

*(***J NICE** *pauses, then...)*

J NICE. You been rhyming this whole year, you still ain't bossed yet/I impregnate your rhymes with poison then bounce/call my shit Offset/I'm a child of the original spitkickers/you ain't hardly that/you talking 'bout Cardi B?/fuck that I'm Cardiac/I got more heart, your whole crew knows I'm a god/see, secretly they voting for me/'cause voting for you is like voter fraud/I break the rules of the master/your ass stay on the plantation/you twelve years a slave/baby I'm Nat Turner/Birth of a Nation/I'm killing your shit like a Panther/and I ain't talking T'Challa/if this was TV/I'd destroy your Empire, with my Power/I got the people's fists raised/singing songs of Glory/your stupid ass rhymes got niggas watching Maury/you ain't real/you a reality show/half fake/you like Dave Chappelle smoking weed/that's why your rhymes sound Half-Baked/I make earthquakes with my poems/while you and your crew try to get high/I'm Maya Angelou of the Cypher/I have no ceiling/still I rise/because my words make the people feel proud/your shit is just absurd/I am the dream of my Ancestors/your ass just a dream deferred.

(The **REBELS** *go crazy.)*

LEAN. J Nice with the Michelle Obama comeback. Makeda went low, J Nice went Woke! You got that one J!

ALANA. Hell naw. That was whack. What's she even talking about?

J NICE. Makeda knows right? Oh, naw you don't. You failed Black History.

EVIDENCE. How you Black and fail Black History??

RAE. You barely passed. Whatchu talking about?

EVIDENCE. I passed though.

ALANA. Lean, her rhyme was whack.

ROK. J Nice came with content. She put Ase on that ass. You ain't got no answer for that! Silence. Siiiiiilence!

(The **REBELS** *look at* **ROK**.*)*

I was just tryna...my bad.

LEAN. J Nice got that. Don't blame me if your girl lost a round. They got one more round to go. This is for the title. So I suggest both of y'all get ready because we ain't stopping until somebody wins.

(The **CREWS** *retreat to their respective sides.)*

ALANA. It's time, Makeda.

MAKEDA. I can do it.

ALANA. Makeda, she straight hit you with the woke facts. How you coming back from that?

MAKEDA. I thought you said she was whack?

ALANA. No, that shit was kinda tight. I passed that Black History test. J Nice was going in.

RAE. Whose side are you on, Alana?

ALANA. You want the bomb now?
MAKEDA. Tell me...

(*Scene shifts to the* **REBELS**.)

EVIDENCE. You gonna have to pull the secret weapon out. Makeda's gonna go hard in the paint.
J NICE. I'll mix and match. Save the bomb for the end.
CHERISH. Whatchu think she has on you?
J NICE. Nothing that can hurt me.
ROK. J Nice?
J NICE. Yeah Rok.

(**ROK** *says nothing.*)

What Rok?
ROK. Well...

(*Shift back to* **MAKEDA'S CREW**.)

MAKEDA. Oh shit!

(**ROK** *hears* **MAKEDA** *and quickly looks at her, knowing what she's discovered.*)

ROK. Jennice, you gotta go last.
J NICE. What?
ROK. This round you should go last.
CHERISH. Rok, that's not how this works. Final round, the challenger goes first.
ROK. You got to, J.
EVIDENCE. Didn't you just hear the rules? If you tryna be down with us, you gotta know the game.
ROK. I know the game. J, I think I should probably...
LEAN. Round Three let's do this!
CHERISH. You got this, J Nice. Rebels coming through with the win. Makeda ain't got nothing for you. Let's drop the bomb on her.
ALANA. Drop the bomb on her, Makeda. J Nice, ain't got nothing for you.

(*The two* **EMCEES** *face each other.*)

LEAN. Here we go, here we go, here we gooooooo! This round will decide who comes out as the true Champion of the South Bronx. Makeda was looking strong in Round One, but J Nice came through in Round Two. Aight, this round right here…better be epic. Y'all ready? Audience y'all ready? Let's get busy!

J NICE. Round Three, I'm taking all crowns within reach/you must think this Popeyes chicken/your ass about to get that two-piece/body, head, body/got you backed up against the ropes/Alana, call up Barack Obama 'cause you friend/she's gonna need Hope/see, these ridiculous lines that I wrote/make your crew wanna sit down and take notes/got you choking and coughing/I'm not sick/baby I'm strep throat/I'm a carnivore/I eat beef/I'm the main chick/you a side-piece/I'm a Prodigy that brings Havoc/my brain is like Mobb Deep/I got God's number on speed dial/all the angels know I'm hot, bro/Death tried to kiss me but I gave his ass Mono/I know the Rebel's coming/that's why you taking steps back/you probably need a hug since you got dumped on Snapchat/and I heard that the reason was he knew you'd lose the crown/that's why he slid up in my DM trying to get my number down/and I might just holla back at him/let him take me to the prom/oh, that means you'll need a date, right?/try Whack Rappers Meet.com.

(The **REBELS** *go crazy.)*

EVIDENCE. Ohhhhhhhhhhhh! J Nice went straight raw this round. Hit her with her own medicine. That's how you finish her!

CHERISH. Like Mortal Kombat son!

EVIDENCE. Lean, just end it now. We done here. Makeda should have a seat and think about the ass whupping she just took!

LEAN. I have never heard the Rebel J Nice go in like that! Aight, Makeda. It's up to you.

(**MAKEDA** *steps forward slowly. She takes a deep breath, then...*)

MAKEDA. J Nice, when we done you gonna wish you stayed home/I'll assassinate you and your crew in one season/Game of Thrones/I use your own force against you/call my style Judo/I skipped you then made you Draw Two/I'm a wild card call me Uno/You a Quarter Water rapper/your best audience? The Bodega/J Nice think she an Alpha female/check this, son…I'm the Omega/I'm gonna end ya/snap my fingers and Poof, kill half of your Avengers/I'll slice you with two machetes/kill you so bad that no one remembers/It's May right now/but you won't be here come September/make you and your three stooges surrender/How many times I gotta tell you J Nice/Makeda runs this shit/plus, that newbie you got there/she a snitch/too thirsty and can't take your hints/so we played on her and she made music like a band instrument/talking about me and my breakup?/dog, you need to wake up/from what I heard, J Nice is a Thot getting her weight up/this conscious shit is phony/just a bunch of woke hype/I heard three boys was training you like the MTA/but no swipes!

J NICE. What the fuck!!

(*She lashes toward* **MAKEDA**. **ALANA** *and* **RAE** *jump in.* **CHERISH** *pulls* **J NICE** *back.*)

I swear to God Makeda! Lemme go!

LEAN. Hold up hold up! What's going on?

J NICE. I'm gonna…

LEAN. Hold up I said!

MAKEDA. What I do?

J NICE. You took it too far! Where did you hear that shit? Where?

CHERISH. Calm down, Jennice!

J NICE. No! You think that shit is funny? You think you can say that about me and I'm supposed to let it go?

CHERISH. J Nice stop! It's just a rhyme! It's not true right?

(**J NICE** *says nothing.*)

Right?

EVIDENCE. Oh shit.

CHERISH. Jennice?

J NICE. You went too far Makeda.

CHERISH. Jennice what happened?

J NICE. There is such a thing as too far. You didn't have to go there. Everything you coulda heard and you went there?

MAKEDA. It's just rhymes.

J NICE. No it isn't! We talk about a lot of shit, but if I found that out about you I would never bring it up in a battle. Not as a woman.

LEAN. Hold up…so some guys really… Makeda you…damn.

(*Silence.*)

J NICE. Just rhymes. They're supposed to be just rhymes. Sticks and stones may break my bones but…rhymes? Rhymes can break your heart. Rhymes can open old wounds. Rhymes can be daggers and if you not careful… naw we not just rhyming. Not me. Not the Rebels. Not y'all.

CHERISH. Jennice…we didn't know. I'm so sorry.

J NICE. Someone knew. Makeda told two truths in that rhyme, didn't you?

EVIDENCE. What? Newbie knew that shit? And you told them?

ROK. I… I didn't know… I wasn't sure why they were asking me…

EVIDENCE. You trying to be down with the Rebels and you telling people's business? You talking to the other side? I knew you were suspect!

ROK. I didn't know! I thought they were trying to recruit me too. They said they heard I was tryna emcee. Said they wanted to know who I was talking to. What I heard. I was thinking it was like an interview. I didn't know. Plus I thought the story wasn't about her… I thought it was like…a myth.

EVIDENCE. You should've known not to be talking to other crews. That's your problem. So thirsty you can't think straight.

ROK. I didn't know if anyone was gonna put me on. But then J Nice did…and it wasn't until today that I knew it was for real.

J NICE. I didn't tell her the whole story. There's always a part people forget. See we spend a lot of time talking about the pain. Yes there was pain. What those boys did to me? I can't even measure that pain. In a lot of ways, that pain is still there, but I never told the story of how I got through. How I came out of the dark place. Cherish remembers when I didn't come to school for two weeks. People thought I was just sick. No. It was this. I never told anyone outside my family the truth. Until last week, Rok. And even then I left names out. But I never told you how I rhymed through my pain. How I found my way back to at least a little bit of myself. You should at least know that part before you delcare yourself the winner Makeda.

(She takes center stage.)

Darkness was closer to me than my own skin/thought it would take me over and cause me to leave my family and friends/I felt like no matter how much I washed, I couldn't clean myself from their sin/over and over again the nightmare played/and I wondered what I did for things to happen that way/were my pants too tight/was my makeup too right/was I sending out signals I didn't intend/was I the one who found enemies amongst friends/how did I go from the life of the party to feeling lifeless/regret and fear had me in their vice grip/I cried on the inside but on the outside I was tight-lipped/think of what people would say/how they'd react/and God I hope this shit don't end up in nobody's rap/I was sure I had met my end, but in that moment an angel walked in/the angel said, "No, your life ain't done"/and she showed me how to rise again like a Sun/she let me cry out my pain 'til my soul was empty/she slayed moments of regret even when those moments were tempting/when I blamed myself/that angel became my lawyer/using the law of the Universe to put things back in order/when I had nothing to say, she let silence be my voice/put a paper and pen in front of me/and gave my words a choice/she lifted my hand as I wrote through my journal/when I focused on the moment/she showed me the eternal/my angel, my mother/my sisters and younger brother/who is too young to understand but used his love to smother/and cover me when my tears felt like rain/and from his arms, somehow I'd make it through each day/but my angel appeared most in these words I'd spit/teaching me to find language to move past regret/giving me a new purpose beyond championships/it's when I kill my own demons that J Nice will be the shit/I'm a Rebel to my own cause/and to the life of my sisters/I'm the reason those who feel like me can finally feel uplifted/see I know how it feels when you ain't sure about your life/but I made it...and am still making it/that's what makes me J Nice.

*(After a moment, **MAKEDA** steps forward.)*

MAKEDA. J Nice...you a way better emcee than I thought...and you damn sure a Shero. I think the crown of the South Bronx belongs to you.

J NICE. I don't really care too much about crowns right now.

MAKEDA. I know, but what you did today...that's more than deserving. Long live the Queen.

*(The two **EMCEES** acknowledge each other. Maybe not by hugging, but definitely with understanding, compassion, and respect.)*

I think we done here.

*(**MAKEDA** and her **CREW** exit.)*

LEAN. J-mutha-freaking-Nice. Man if this was an after-school special there'd be like some mad important message right now. But I don't think it needs to be said, you know? Congrats.

(**LEAN** *exits.*)

EVIDENCE. Anything we can do? I got family that works with young women who been through things like this. Whatever you need, I got you.

J NICE. I appreciate that.

CHERISH. We appreciate you. Don't ever feel like you can't call us. We got you... Rebels always win.

J NICE. No doubt.

EVIDENCE. Whatchu wanna do about Suspect Sally over here?

J NICE. Gimme a minute with her.

EVIDENCE. We'll be outside.

(**EVIDENCE** *and* **CHERISH** *exit.*)

ROK. J Nice I am so...

J NICE. I know you new to the rap game. Nobody blames you for not knowing. Hopefully you understand that being an emcee is more than just having bars. Some of us do this for our lives.

ROK. I get that.

J NICE. I think it's gonna take you a minute before you ready to rock with us...or any crew for that matter. People may not be feeling you for a minute.

ROK. I know.

J NICE. Know what you can do?

ROK. What?

J NICE. Write for your life. Don't write to kill a rapper in the Cypher. That shit ain't what's really important. Write for your life.

(*She leaves.* **ROK** *is alone for a moment.*)

ROK. Ase.

(*Lights out.*)

End of Play

CITIZENS UNITED

A comedy about the end of American democracy

well, not the end but a pretty drastic assault

that came from within

by five people

who can't be voted out

five men

who will keep that job till they quit or die

though granted

one of them is already

dead

Kate Cortesi

CITIZENS UNITED was first produced at Theatre Row in New York City from May 17–19, 2019. The production was directed by Heather Lanza. The cast was as follows:

HOPE OF	Gabriela Alexa Centeno
THE FUTURE	Ibiana Collado
DAVID BOSSIE / SONIA SOTOMAYOR	Kiara Jorge
F.E.C. / CLARENCE THOMAS	Taniya Harrison
VLAD / MALCOLM STEWART	Lauren A. Wood
JOHN ROBERTS	Gabriella (Ella) Derke
JOHN PAUL STEVENS	Mars Taska
DAVID SOUTER	Shoshana E. Hoover
ANTONIN SCALIA	Vivien Baker
RUTH BADER GINSBURG	Stephanie Lane
ANTHONY KENNEDY	Ava Cairl
STEPHEN BREYER	Megan Fishman
TED OLSON	Jordan Elizabeth Ori

CHARACTERS

All characters can be played by actors of any race/gender, except Ruth Bader Ginsburg, who should be played by a female-identifying student.

HOPE OF – A teenager. A natural student.

THE FUTURE – A teenager. A natural teacher.

DAVID BOSSIE – The white, male, middle-aged president of Citizens United, a right-wing advocacy group that makes ads and documentaries for conservative causes.

F.E.C. – The Federal Election Commission, a government agency that enforces campaign finance law, personified in this play by a loud charismatic person.

VLAD – A teenage boy from Russia who wants to help The Future win a student government election.

JOHN ROBERTS – The Chief Justice of the Supreme Court. A white man, young relative to the other Justices, votes conservative.

JOHN PAUL STEVENS – An Associate Justice of the Supreme Court. An old white man. Wrote the dissent in *Citizens United v. F.E.C.*, votes liberal.

DAVID SOUTER – An Associate Justice of the Supreme Court. An old white man. Votes liberal.

ANTONIN SCALIA – An Associate Justice of the Supreme Court. An old, white, Italian-American man. Votes very conservative.

RUTH BADER GINSBURG – An Associate Justice of the Supreme Court. A very old, white, Jewish woman. Votes liberal.

CLARENCE THOMAS – An Associate Justice of the Supreme Court. An old black man. Votes very conservative.

SAMUEL ALITO – An Associate Justice of the Supreme Court. An old, white, Italian-American man. Votes very conservative.

ANTHONY KENNEDY – An Associate Justice of the Supreme Court. An old white man. Votes along conservative lines but is often the so-called "swing vote" when the conservative and liberal Justices split 4-4, which is the case in this story.

STEPHEN BREYER – An Associate Justice of the Supreme Court. An old white man. Votes liberal.

TED OLSON – A fancy lawyer who represents Citizen United before the Supreme Court. A middle-aged white man.

MALCOLM STEWART – The Deputy Solicitor General for the United States, which just means a fancy government lawyer. He represents the government before the Supreme Court. A middle-aged white man.

SONIA SOTOMAYOR – An Associate Justice of the Supreme Court, whose first Supreme Court hearing was the second *Citizens United v. F.E.C.* oral argument in September 2009. The first Latinx Supreme Court Justice, nominated by Barack Obama to replace Justice Souter.

SETTING

The Supreme Court, mostly. And the theater, always.

TIME

A tale from 2009 is being narrated by the bright youth of today.

AUTHOR'S NOTES

This play is probably best performed by people who are teenagers. It's less painful when the messengers are the youth.

Note on Pronouns:

An exciting thing about this play is how fluid the casting can be. People of any race and gender identity can play these characters, even though the majority of the actual historical figures represented are white cis-gendered men. In the case of the "real life" characters, the script will use the pronouns of the historical figures, regardless of the gender of the actor.

Three characters are not historical figures: Hope Of, The Future, and F.E.C. The script will refer to these characters as "she," to honor the original cast members, but your production should feel free to change these pronouns to suit your actors.

(Loud, nightmarish, overlapping criticisms of Hillary Clinton fill the theater: "She's untrustworthy," "Unfit for office," "There's just something about her I don't like," etc.)

*(At the door, in a nice suit, is **DAVID BOSSIE**, the president of a non-profit called Citizens United. He greets the audience as they enter, shaking hands, welcoming, schmoozing...)*

BOSSIE. David Bossie, president of Citizens United, welcome to *Hillary: The Movie*, so glad you could join us. Hi! I'm David Bossie. *(Etc.)*

*(Once the audience is mostly seated, someone in a less-nice suit barges in. This is the **F.E.C.**)*

F.E.C. Cut it off. Cut it off. Cut the movie off now! And cut those cell phones off while you're at it. No, I do not mean put them on *vibrate*. Off, *OFF*!

BOSSIE. Who are you?

F.E.C. I am the F.E.C. And you, sir, are breaking campaign finance law.

BOSSIE. What? This is an educational ninety-minute documentary!

F.E.C. Documentary my asterisk. This is an advertisement with one message and one message only: "Don't Vote For Hillary."

There's a word for that kind of ad. You know what that word is?

BOSSIE. Helpful?

F.E.C. *Electioneering*. And electioneering by a corporation like you sixty days before an election is *a felony*, as per Section 203 of the Bipartisan Campaign Reform Act.

BOSSIE. You're freaking kidding.

F.E.C. I never freaking kid about Section 203 of the Bipartisan Campaign Reform Act.

> *(A pause.)*

BOSSIE. Fine. *(To the projectionist.)* Cut it off.

> *(Satisfied, the* **F.E.C.** *heads off.)*

But mark my words, F.E.C. You've not heard the last of Citizens United! *[It echoes: "Citizens United, Citizens United…"]*

> *(A shift.* **BOSSIE** *is gone. Onstage, in front of the still-closed curtain, a teenager we shall refer to as* **HOPE OF** *steps out, looks around, and beckons another teenager,* **THE FUTURE***, to follow.)*

HOPE OF. *(To the audience.)* Good evening, everyone.

> *(No answer or too soft.)*

Good evening, everyone.

> *(The audience responds with "Good evening," "Hello," etc.)*

That's better.

THE FUTURE. Welcome to our play! *Citizens United*! My name is The Future, and this is my friend –

HOPE OF. Hope Of. *(Pointing to self.)* Hope Of.

THE FUTURE. *(Pointing to self.)* The Future.

HOPE OF. Hi.

Welcome to Citizens United!

THE FUTURE. A new play by Kate Cortesi.

HOPE OF. Performed by *us*, an acting troop of beautiful geniuses from *[insert your hometown or city, or "the Tri-State Area"]*.

THE FUTURE. Produced by *[insert your producing entity]*.

HOPE OF. With loving emotional support –

THE FUTURE. And *financial* support –

HOPE OF & THE FUTURE. From y'all.

HOPE OF. And we thank you.

Before we start, let's go over a few *terms* –

THE FUTURE. *Concepts* –

HOPE OF. Constitutional *amendments* –

THE FUTURE. Congressional *statutes*. Because if you know enough to follow along, this play is –

HOPE OF. Really fun!

THE FUTURE. But if you don't, it's –

HOPE OF. Kinda boring.

> *(A stack of flashcards appears.* **THE FUTURE** *holds one up: THE FIRST AMENDMENT.)*

THE FUTURE. What is *the First Amendment*?
(When no one answers.) Not doing this for my health, people. The First Amendment.

HOPE OF. *(Prompting them.)* Freedom of blank.

> *(The audience responds with "Speech," hopefully.)*

THE FUTURE. Thank you Jesus yes. Freedom of Speech!

HOPE OF & THE FUTURE. Congress shall make no law *abridging the freedom of speech*.

THE FUTURE. The First Amendment also covers freedom of religion and the press but today, we're talking about *speech*.

HOPE OF. *(To* **THE FUTURE.***)* Why was freedom of speech important to the framers?

THE FUTURE. Because language is how we share *ideas*. If Congress can restrict speech, it can censor *ideas*. And the framers thought that's something a mean old tyrant like King George would do, not a hip young democracy like America.

HOPE OF. And now we can say whatever we want, the end?

THE FUTURE. Well, *no*. There are actually quite a few exceptions. For example, you can't use curse words on the radio or network TV. It's illegal to urge a crowd to start rioting...

HOPE OF. So, "Congress shall make no law abridging freedom of speech," except sometimes?

THE FUTURE. Exactly.

HOPE OF. Freedom of speech is *debatable*.

THE FUTURE. *Literally* debatable. Which is why we're here today. To debate freedom of speech.

(The F.E.C. is suddenly back.)

F.E.C. Great! Let's debate it.

HOPE OF. Oh, hi F.E.C.

F.E.C. *(To HOPE OF.)* Hi.

HOPE OF. The Federal Election Commission is back.

F.E.C. *(To the audience.)* Hi.

To debate this, we need to talk about the other side. Y'all are up here, "First Amendment this, First Amendment that." Which is great. But there's another value we need to educate them about.

HOPE OF. What's that?

F.E.C. Fairness. Equality. Specifically, fairness and equality in *elections*.

(The F.E.C. takes the index cards from THE FUTURE, flips through them, and holds up: BIPARTISAN CAMPAIGN REFORM ACT.)

What is the Bipartisan Campaign Reform Act? Sometimes written like this:

(Flips it over.) BCRA.

You pronounce this Bickruh. *Bickruh!*

HOPE OF & THE FUTURE. Bickruh.

F.E.C. BCRA is a *law* passed by Congress in 2003 about money in elections.

Why did Congress pass this law? Why do we need BCRA? Okay. Let's say Hope Of and The Future are running for student government president.

(Now HOPE OF and THE FUTURE are two high-schoolers running for office.)

THE FUTURE. I am the best and Hope Of is the worst!

HOPE OF. No *I* am the best and The *Future* is the worst!

F.E.C. The school gives both of them a hundred posters to campaign with, because it wants the campaign to be free and fair:
Free – you can write whatever you want on your posters.
Fair – everyone gets the same number of posters.
What you can say, that's not controlled, that's free.
But how many posters you get, that is controlled, because that's fair.

(VLAD enters with a massive stack of glossy, colorful posters. He has a Russian accent.)

VLAD. Psst! The Future. Hello.

F.E.C. Fair until *Vlad* comes along. Vlad from *[insert nearby wealthy town or neighborhood]*.

VLAD. I make *thousands* of posters. For you. Bright color. Very big. See? *(Showing the poster.)* Hope Of is poop. *[poop emoji]* Vote for The Future. Is great shot of you, no?

(We may see a billboard-sized projection of one of Vlad's posters.)

F.E.C. Vlad gets involved in the school election.

VLAD. As volunteer! You pay nothing! I put big posters in subway. On bus. I make beautiful billboard over *[insert local public spot]*. You watch. She will be losing and you will be winning.

F.E.C. Sure enough, Hope Of loses.

HOPE OF. *(Crying.)* I'm not poop! Lies! It's all lies!

F.E.C. And The Future is student president.

THE FUTURE. Yes!
I didn't cheat, did I? This nice Russian man just wanted to help, out of the kindness of his heart.

VLAD. Of course. But story is not finish. After election, is time for how you say? *Prom*. And you, my old friend, will hire *me* for all prom business, soup to nuts.

THE FUTURE. Uh, cool. Do you have a portfolio? And a reference I can present to the student council? We make decisions by vote.

VLAD. Try again my friend.

(**THE FUTURE** *is confused.*)

I make you president, you make me *prom czar*.

THE FUTURE. I don't feel comfortable with that.

VLAD. Too bad. *You owe me.*

(*Pause.*)

Don't worry. I have authentic Russian disco ball.

(*He is gone.*)

HOPE OF. (*Picking up an election poster.*) There's a word for speech like these posters. The F.E.C. was shouting it at the start of the show, about *Hillary: The Movie*.

(**THE FUTURE** *holds up an index card:* ELECTIONEERING.)

HOPE OF & THE FUTURE. Electioneering.

HOPE OF. "Vote for The Future." "Don't vote Hope Of." Ads that tell you how to vote. That's electioneering.

THE FUTURE. And *electioneering* by *corporations* is illegal right before an election, according to that law:

(*She holds up the BCRA index card.*)

HOPE OF & THE FUTURE. BCRA.

HOPE OF. BCRA was created to stop that Vlad-prom situation.

F.E.C. Make sense?

(*Hopefully the audience says "Yes."*)

Great. So that's *my* side. Thank you for listening. It means a lot.

HOPE OF. Hold up. I have a question. The First Amendment does say Congress shall make no law abridging freedom of speech. But: "Vote for John" – that's political speech, right? Doesn't BCRA go against the First Amendment?

F.E.C. Congress said no. Congress, and in the past, the Supreme Court, said advertisements aren't political speech, they're advertisements.

HOPE OF. Ooh. Subtle difference.

F.E.C. Subtle, but hella important.
(Giving the audience the eye.) I'm out.

*(The **F.E.C.** exits.)*

THE FUTURE. *(To **HOPE OF**.)* You know, for a government regulator, she's all right.
(To the audience.) Okay so Hope Of's question, does BCRA go against the First Amendment, is actually the heart of Citizens United's case.

HOPE OF. The company Citizens United is saying *Hillary: The Movie* is political speech protected by the First Amendment.

THE FUTURE. And the F.E.C. – the government – says *Hillary: The Movie* is electioneering, and therefore banned by BCRA from airing sixty days before an election.

HOPE OF. Okay. Who decides who's right?

(They start to draw the curtains.)

THE FUTURE. I dunno, Hope Of. Is there an *entire branch of government* dedicated to interpreting the Constitution?

HOPE OF. I dunno, is there?

(A beat drops* as the curtain reveals nine Justices: **ANTONIN SCALIA, CLARENCE THOMAS, SAMUEL ALITO, JOHN PAUL STEVENS, ANTHONY KENNEDY, RUTH BADER GINSBURG, DAVID SOUTER, STEPHEN BREYER,** *and in the middle, Chief Justice* **JOHN ROBERTS**.*)*

(To the audience.) Are you ready?

THE FUTURE. She *said*: Y'ALL READY?

---

*A license to produce *Citizens United* does not include a performance license for any third-party or copyrighted music. Licensees should create an original composition or use music in the public domain. For further information, please see Music Use Note on page 3.

(When the audience is good and hyped:)

THE FUTURE. Mr. Chief Justice, your honors, take it away.
Deliberate on how it went down that day.

JOHN ROBERTS. Ladies and gentlemen, you could be anywhere tonight, but you chose to be here, with us, at the Supreme Court in Washington, D.C. I'd like to introduce myself and my fellow Justices! Why don't we go around, say our names, the year we joined the Court, and the president who appointed us, as well as something fun about ourselves. Stevens, you've been here the longest, why don't you start.

JOHN PAUL STEVENS.

My name is John Paul Stevens, I was thrown into this mix in
1970 by Richard "Dick" Nixon
Sure my roots shoot from the conservative faction
But I scoot left on Affirmative Action.

ANTONIN SCALIA.

I'm Antonin Scalia see ya wouldn't wanna be ya
Reagan, '88, is the guy who put me here *[rhymes with "be ya"]*
Italian from Queens I like going to the Opera
Start to say the Constitution's living I'mma stop ya.

ANTHONY KENNEDY.

Anthony Kennedy, same year same dude
I'm the swing vote, bro, so don't give me attitude
And I'm the middle of the nine, but I vote pretty conservative
Change or stay the same? I'm like, please add preservatives.

CLARENCE THOMAS.

Clarence Thomas. I do the right thing.
Right like, "not left." Right like, "right wing."
I vote right of him, vote right of him too.
My confirmation hearing – we don't need to get into.
Folks try to hate but ain't no Justice sweeta,
Ask him, him, or him. Just please don't ask Anita.

JOHN ROBERTS.
>John Roberts, sorry to cut you off
>But not really 'cause I'm Chief and ya motherloving boss.
>Dub put me here, and I step to the right
>But a coupla deviations made the right ignite
>against me. Voted for Obamacare, gay rights too
>Nominee reined in by jurispru–
>dence. So y'all don't know what I'm 'bout to do
>I mean you do. But. There's a doubt, or two.

SAMUEL ALITO.
>Sam Alito, same president as *him*
>here since "SexyBack" was number one and Posh was settin' trends
>Yeah you know the year, two thousand and six
>I'm Italian from Brooklyn and Conservative as sh**.

STEPHEN BREYER.
>Stephen Breyer *[rhymes with "fire"]*
>I leapt into this fire
>Because William Jeff Clinton said that I'm the guy to hire.

RUTH BADER GINSBURG.
>It was also Bill C who said, "You're the judge for me,"
>Ruth Bader Ginsburg, y'all, 1993!
>Don't call me Mrs., it's Your Honor if you please,
>But *if* you feelin' nasty it's Notorious R.B.G.!

JOHN ROBERTS. Great, is that all nine? –

DAVID SOUTER.
>– Just about, Mr. Chief Justice
>But I think that you just skipped me 'cause you know that you can't touch this.
>My name is David Souter, I like ridin' on my boat
>up north, but in *DC* let me clear my throat ah-hunh
>Put up here by Bush the daddy dad
>But I vote to the left so the right is very mad
>at me. Don't talk much, but when I do I say a lot
>So don't skip me again because I ain't gone yet (mother –)

(As the outro music plays,* Citizens United's **DAVID BOSSIE** *steps out, hyped, like before a boxing match.)*

BOSSIE. I said you'd not heard the last from us and here we are. That's right, that's *right*.
(To the audience.) Instead of waiting for the F.E.C. to come for us, we came for the F.E.C.

*(***TED OLSON*** takes the stage with a bit too much confidence.)*

OLSON. Hi. I'm Ted, a very good, *very expensive* lawyer.

BOSSIE. Y'all messed with the wrong non-profit's First Amendment rights.

(He gives **OLSON** *a shoulder rub and maybe even squirts water into his mouth like a boxing coach.)*

ROBERTS. We will hear arguments today in Case 08-205, Citizens United versus The Federal Election Commission.

HOPE OF. Supreme Court 101. Each oral argument lasts one hour. Each side gets thirty minutes. That's it.

THE FUTURE. Like a TV show, except live.

HOPE OF. Lawyers who argue before the Supreme Court are the best in the field – *and* – standing before these nine Justices is extremely intimidating.

THE FUTURE. They're scared as hell.

HOPE OF. Ladies and gentlemen, the lawyer for Citizens United, Theodore Olson.

OLSON. *(To the audience, really suave.)* Good evening. You enjoying the show so far?
I'm so glad.

(A beat drops as **OLSON** *starts to rap.*)*

---

*A license to produce *Citizens United* does not include a performance license for any third-party or copyrighted music. Licensees should create an original composition or use music in the public domain. For further information, please see Music Use Note on page 3.

My name is Theodore Olson, but you can call me Ted
I'm a freaking good lawyer so I cost a lot of bread.

ROBERTS. Mr. Olson?

(Record scratch. The beat stops.)

You have thirty minutes.

OLSON. Right. Thank you Mr. Chief Justice and may it please the court.

Participation in the political process is the First Amendment's most fundamental guarantee. Yet that freedom is being smothered by a tyrannical federal agency.

THE FUTURE. Ted goes on to explain it's a –

OLSON. *Felony –*

THE FUTURE. For a –

OLSON. *Small non-profit –*

THE FUTURE. To air a ninety-minute documentary about –

OLSON. Hillary Clinton, a candidate for the nation's highest office!

HOPE OF. And he's extra pissed because other companies *are* allowed to broadcast the movie –

OLSON. NPR! Fox News! Nickelodeon!

HOPE OF. Because they're *"media."* The media *can* say this stuff.

THE FUTURE. But if Citizens United does it?

OLSON. The producers *face five years in prison*.

SCALIA. Five years?

OLSON. For *each* Pay-Per-View download! For each *ad* for the movie.

ALITO. Oh dang. That's a long time in jail.

GINSBURG. Well, *Hillary: The Movie* is in effect an ad that says, "Don't vote for Hillary." That's electioneering.

OLSON. We disagree, Justice Ginsburg. *Hillary: The Movie* is *political speech*, the very *core* of the First Amendment. The government needs a *really really good reason* to throw people in jail for airing a *ninety-minute documentary*.

HOPE OF. You hear that a lot in his argument. Ninety-minute documentary.

OLSON. Ninety-minute documentary! Ninety-minute documentary.

THE FUTURE. And Olson says the government doesn't have a *really really* good reason for banning it.

OLSON. They don't!

HOPE OF. But Souter and Ginsburg are all over him.

SOUTER. If this message is so key to the political process, it *can* be broadcast, Mr. Olson – just not by Citizens United! It can go on TV, as long as it's paid for by the candidate's PAC *[pronounced "pack"]*.

THE FUTURE. PAC. That's P-A-C, which stands for Political Action Committee. Each candidate has to officially establish their own PAC to run for office. And PAC *money* is regulated by BCRA, too. To keep things fair.

HOPE OF. Like the school giving us the same number of posters, and letting us put them up in the same places.

SOUTER. BCRA does permit your message on their airwaves, but the *campaign itself* would have to broadcast it. BCRA's issue is with *your* company, with *unlimited sums* of money, airing this movie. Because if the other candidates don't have all that money, the race is unfair, and *money* dominates our political process. That's the situation we want to avoid, right? Elections going to the highest spender?

OLSON. Citizens United is a *small non-profit*.

SOUTER. Ah. So if your movie were paid for by, say, General Electric, it would be a violation. But you're okay because you're such a cute little organization?

OLSON. I mean, I *am* cute.

GINSBURG. Mr. Olson, isn't it true that when the government asked for your donor list, to see *who exactly* was providing all this money to criticize Ms. Clinton, you didn't provide it?

OLSON. Didn't we?

GINSBURG. No, you didn't.

OLSON. We meant to.

GINSBURG. Airing *Hillary: The Movie* on Pay-Per-View costs over a million dollars, and you all didn't tell the F.E.C. *whose* million it was! Don't you think the American people deserve to know who pays for their leaders' election campaigns?

HOPE OF. Ginsburg points out a major reason we have campaign finance laws in the first place: so we *know* who's paying our leaders' electioneering bills.

So we know who they owe.

GINSBURG. If candidates are funded by small donations from American citizens, they'll "owe" American citizens.

HOPE OF. But if it's the NRA, US Steel, or you know, Russian billionaires –

GINSBURG. They might feel a certain loyalty to the NRA, US Steel, or Russian billionaires!

THE FUTURE. Then Ginsburg pivots back to the ninety-minute thing.

GINSBURG. I'd like to go back to your ninety-minute point.

OLSON. Wonderful.

GINSBURG. You're saying that the *length* of your movie makes it okay.

OLSON. It's a ninety-minute documentary! It's *not* those quick flashy ads BCRA was concerned about.

GINSBURG. But if your movie said, "Don't vote for Hillary," over and over, for ninety minutes, it *would* be one of those ads, right? A really long one?

OLSON. But it doesn't say that. It's researched, it's thorough –

SOUTER. Here in the government's brief, I'm on page nineteen, it quotes your movie, "She will lie about anything. She is deceitful. She is ruthless, cunning, dishonest, do anything for power, will speak dishonestly, reckless, a congenital liar, sorely lacking in qualifications, not qualified as commander in chief." I mean, this is not the *New York*

Times, counselor, and it's not a comedic stage play that students can perform. This is electioneering. It's ninety minutes of *Don't Vote For Hillary*.

OLSON. Our movie educates, it informs –

ROBERTS. Thank you so much counselor, you're out of time.

HOPE OF. Then it's the F.E.C.'s turn. The government, defending BCRA, and its restrictions on airing *Hillary: The Movie*.

MALCOLM STEWART. *(Coming through the audience, shaking hands.)* Hello. Good evening. I love that sweater, it brings out your eyes. *(Etc.)*

ROBERTS. And arguing on behalf of the government, Malcolm Stewart, Deputy Attorney General –

STEWART. *(To an audience member.)* That's the third highest government lawyer in America. Two guys above me. That's it. And they're overdue to retire but you didn't hear that from me.

ROBERTS. Counselor, you have thirty minutes.

HOPE OF. Stewart's also very nervous but does his best to hide it.

STEWART. Thank you Mr. Chief Justice and may it pees – pees – the court. Not pees, *pees*. I mean *please*. I don't know why I keeps saying pees. I don't even have to pee!

(Clears his throat.)

The government and the citizens of the United States have a vested interest in elections that are democratic and fair.

HOPE OF. Malcolm Stewart basically repeats what Souter and Ginsburg said. It's not about *what's* being said, it's about *who's* saying it, and how much money they have.

THE FUTURE. The government *does have* a really really good reason to penalize electioneering. That reason? *Fairness* and *equality* in election races.

HOPE OF. And how do we know this is a good reason, he asks.

STEWART. Look what happened before election finance laws existed. The winner was the guy with the most money who could out-advertise his opponents.

HOPE OF. That's code for: the rich white guy with the rich white friends.

THE FUTURE. The argument seems to be going pretty well for Malcolm, when two Justices start testing the boundaries of what BCRA can regulate.

KENNEDY. Counselor, if *Hillary: The Movie*, and ads for *Hillary: The Movie*, can be banned sixty days before an election, what *else* does BCRA consider contraband?

STEWART. I'm not sure what you mean, Justice Kennedy.

KENNEDY. If this movie were a book, could BCRA jail its publishers for selling it before an election?

STEWART. That would depend on if the book is electioneering.

KENNEDY. If it's a 200-page book, and on the last page it says, "Vote For John," that's electioneering, right?

STEWART. Well, that depends on who paid for the book.

SCALIA. If Citizens United paid for the publication of the book, and on the last page it says, "Vote For John," can the government ban the book?

STEWART. Well, I suppose, for that *narrow* window of time right before a primary or an election –

ROBERTS. So your answer is yes.

STEWART. Uhhhhh – wait what?

ROBERTS. If Citizens United pays for the publication of a book that's 200 pages long, and at the end it says, in print, "Vote For John," your position is, that book can be banned right before an election, under penalty of five years in prison. Yes or no?

(Dramatic pause.)

THE FUTURE. This is the moment Malcom Stewart still has nightmares about.

STEWART. I suppose; if the book were published by a non-media corporation, and it were being sold in that small window right before an election, then yes, sure, the government's position is that the book could be banned. The Court / has ruled before in –

THE FUTURE. He said it. The book could be banned.

HOPE OF. The book could be banned.

THE FUTURE. That's a big deal.

STEWART. I said the book could be banned.

> *(All nine **JUSTICES** repeat, in a kind of nightmare chorus:)*

ALL JUSTICES.

He said the book could be banned.

He said the book could be banned.

The book could be banned. *(Etc.)*

> *(During this, the courtroom changes dramatically. Maybe we remix parts of the argument in a nightmare soundscape as the courtroom transforms into the innermost Supreme Court back chamber. **STEWART** stands in the middle, trying to rescue his argument.)*

STEWART. You guys are totally missing the point! This isn't about book-banning, or locking people up for political thoughts. This is about a narrow application of the law, created by the Congress of the United States of America to stop our democracy from being sold to the highest bidder! Guys? Hello?

> *(He is alone, defeated.)*

Oh, shitake mushrooms.

HOPE OF. Sucks dude.

> *(We are now in the innermost sanctum of the Supreme Court: the Justices' Conference Room.)*

> *(**HOPE OF** and **THE FUTURE** step forward. All the **JUSTICES** take their seats around the table, except **GINSBURG**, who is doing push-ups off to the side.)*

After oral arguments, the Justices adjourn to the innermost sanctum of the Supreme Court.

THE FUTURE. The girls' bathroom.

HOPE OF. The Justices' *Conference Room*. The room where it happens. No one is allowed in here except the Justices.

THE FUTURE. Here, they discuss the cases of the day and the Chief Justice takes a preliminary vote.

ROBERTS. *(To* **SCALIA.***)* Tony, get your feet off the table.

So. That was fun, huh? What do you guys think, does Citizens United have a case?

SOUTER. No. Definitely not.

BREYER. Noperoni Pizza

STEVENS. With extra nope.

(**BREYER** *and* **STEVENS** *high five.*)

ROBERTS. Ruth?

GINSBURG. *(Last three push-ups.)* Ninety-eight…ninety-nine…100. *(Springing to her feet.)* Do they have a *case*?! Let me ask you this, John: Do we want our leaders chosen by the richest advertisers? Congress doesn't, the American people don't, and neither do I. So no, hell no! Citizens United does not have a case!

ROBERTS. Thank you, Ruth. *I* think Citizens United *does* have a case.

Gentlemen?

THOMAS, ALITO & SCALIA. They have a case.

THE FUTURE. This is a familiar situation. The four liberal Justices on one side, the four conservative Justices on the other. When this happens, all attention turns to –

KENNEDY. Who, me?

THE FUTURE. Anthony Kennedy.

KENNEDY. Hello.

HOPE OF. The swing vote.

KENNEDY. *(Loves being called this.)* Oh no *please* don't call me that, I hate it.

(Pause.)

What did you call me?

EVERYONE ELSE. The Swing Vote.

KENNEDY. That's a *terrible* thing to say! If *I'm* the swing vote in landmark cases that affect *everyone* in America, it means the only vote that matters is *mine*, which makes *me*...

EVERYONE ELSE. The most powerful man in America.

KENNEDY. Stop! I'm not the most powerful man in America. Please stop saying I'M THE MOST POWERFUL MAN IN AMERICA!

ROBERTS. Anthony. What do you think?

KENNEDY. That I am certainly not the most powerful –

ROBERTS. About Citizens United.

KENNEDY. What about it?

ROBERTS. Do you agree with Citizens? That *Hillary: The Movie* is a legitimate documentary, so they can show it before an election under the First Amendment? *Or* do you agree with the F.E.C., that this movie is electioneering and is thus subject to BCRA?

KENNEDY. The first one. No the second one. No the first one. No the second one. Neither? JK that's not an option give me a sec.

Hm.

> *(Pause.)*

Hmmmmmmmmmm.

I think...that...Citizens United...is...

HOPE OF. *(To the audience.)* What do you think he says?

KENNEDY. Grab your popcorn, kids, 'cause we're going to the movies!

Team Citizens United!

> *(The **CONSERVATIVE JUSTICES** cheer. The **LIBERAL JUSTICES** boo. They should try to get the audience to participate in this. If this goes well, **HOPE OF** and **THE FUTURE** settle everyone down.)*

HOPE OF. When the Court is split, one Justice writes the opinion of the majority.

ROBERTS. Me! I'm writing the opinion of the Court on this one. Me. John Roberts. I'm the boss. Hi.

HOPE OF. And one of the *dissenting Justices*, the ones who disagree with the majority, writes a *dissenting opinion*.

*(**SOUTER** clears his throat.)*

SOUTER. I wouldn't mind tackling this one.

STEVENS. Souter it is.

HOPE OF. So, Chief Justice Roberts goes to his chambers to write the opinion of the Court. And Justice Souter goes to his to write the dissent. But then…something strange happens.

*(**ROBERTS** and **SOUTER** are pulled by Supreme forces to opposite ends of the stage to write their opinions. The company splits; the conservative half hangs around **ROBERTS**, while the liberal half hangs around **SOUTER**. **KENNEDY** remains center stage, in neither camp.)*

KENNEDY. *(To the audience.)* As John writes that *Hillary: The Movie* is First Amendment speech, and David writes that it's not, I feel…*unresolved*. So I go write my own concurring opinion.

THE FUTURE. A concurring opinion is when you agree with the majority but for a different reason.

ROBERTS. *(Writing as he types.)* In conclusion –

SOUTER. *(Same.)* In conclusion –

ROBERTS. The Court thinks that *Hillary: The Movie* is the kind of political debate that the founders wrote the First Amendment to protect.

SOUTER. *Hillary: The Movie* is not robust political debate, it's a long corporate-sponsored advertisement. It's electioneering.

ROBERTS. Those who dislike the movie's message can respond with their own speech. That's how political debate works.

SOUTER. 300 members of Congress found the effects of money in advertising on elections *un*democratic. The four dissenting members of this Court don't presume to know better.

ROBERTS. *(Pulling his decision from the typewriter.)* So says the Court.

SOUTER. Ruth, Steven, John Paul? Ready to sign?

ROBERTS. Guys?

> *(But the signers are stopped by a noise. The click-clack-clacking of a typewriter.)*

SCALIA. What's that?

THOMAS. Kennedy. Writing a concurring opinion.

ALITO. Ooh! What do you think it says?

> *(**KENNEDY** rips his own opinion from his own typewriter.)*

KENNEDY. Citizens United can screen and advertise *Hillary: The Movie*, whenever it wants! It's just speech. Is it sophisticated, or even accurate? Who cares! The Constitution does not say Congress shall not abridge freedom of high-quality, nuanced statements – it says *speech*. It doesn't distinguish between good speech and bad. It's all speech. There's no such thing as too much speech. *Hillary: The Movie* is fine. It's BCRA that's unconstitutional.

THOMAS. *(Liking the sound of this.)* It's BCRA that's unconstitutional?

GINSBURG. Anthony wants to strike down BCRA, God help us.

THOMAS. *(Excited.)* Anthony wants to *strike down* BCRA!

SCALIA. *(Excited.)* Overturning BCRA. I never thought of that!

STEVENS. For the *middle* of the nine, he sure is going to extremes.

SOUTER. *(Quiet, livid.)* Look out, friends. However extreme an idea sounds, once it's been uttered, it can happen.

ROBERTS. *(Looking over his opinion.)* Huh. Kennedy wants to strike down BCRA.

ALITO. I mean, do you kinda *love* it?

> *(***SCALIA***,* **THOMAS***, and* **ALITO** *run over to* **KENNEDY***.)*

THOMAS. John, love ya bro, but I'm joining the concurrence.

ALITO. Samesies!

SCALIA. Same same same!

HOPE OF. Uh-oh. Looks like the majority opinion isn't the majority opinion anymore.

SOUTER. What did I tell you. Once it's been uttered, it can happen.

KENNEDY. *I hate being called the most powerful man in America.*

> *(***ROBERTS** *stands slowly. What's happening is big.)*

ROBERTS. All right. I reassign the Court's opinion to: Anthony Kennedy.

> *(The* **LIBERAL JUSTICES** *look to* **KENNEDY** *with disappointment and disgust.)*
>
> *(***KENNEDY***, ever eager to be popular, stands to defend himself.)*

KENNEDY. Guys! C'mon. Don't look at me like that. Tell me! Why aren't ads about politicians political speech? "Don't Vote for Hillary." That's about as political as political speech gets?

STEVENS. Congress prohibits marketing cigarettes to minors, and we allow it. Those ads are illegal. We restrict *that* freedom of speech. Why? Because we know, marketing cigarettes to kids means more kids smoke. And smoking kills people. Calling electioneering political speech is like calling a Marlboro ad a public health debate. Marlboro isn't raising awareness. It's buying an outcome.

KENNEDY. Well, John Paul, I think that's an *interesting debate*. Punch it up, put it on TV, and we'll throw a First Amendment party at my place!

BREYER. I don't understand: In this case, *whose* free speech was infringed on? The president of Citizens United David Bossie can say whatever he wants about Hillary Clinton or any other candidate. Same with their board members, their camera man, their janitor. They can all shout their opinions on Hillary Clinton from the rooftops, and BCRA is *fine* with that! All BCRA is saying, is that a *corporate treasury* can't *pay for* TV and radio time, right before an election. Paying for ads is not the same as an individual's right to speak.

KENNEY. Do we give up our individual rights when we band together and incorporate? Are corporations not just collections of individuals?

GINSBURG. Sure, Anthony. Corporations are people too. That's very funny.

> (*The* **CONSERVATIVE JUSTICES** *like the sound of that.*)

KENNEDY. Yeah. Exactly. Corporations are people too.

> (*Through the following, the* **JUSTICES** *clear the stage, except for* **ROBERTS**, *who is alone in his chambers, and* **SOUTER**, *who stands at Roberts' door.*)

> (**SOUTER** *knocks on Roberts' door.*)

SOUTER. Mr. Chief Justice.

ROBERTS. Come in. David! Hello.

> (**SOUTER** *puts a multi-page document on Roberts' desk.*)

SOUTER. I've rewritten my dissent. It's –

ROBERTS. Longer.

SOUTER. Yes.

ROBERTS. Thank you.

> (**SOUTER** *moves to leave.*)

What are the – highlights?

> (**SOUTER** *takes a moment to consider the question. Finally, he turns back to his boss.*)

SOUTER. Mr. Chief Justice.

ROBERTS. We're friends. Call me John.

SOUTER. Mr. Chief Justice. In this ruling, the majority, a *fragile* majority, has taken a narrow question about a narrow application of the law, a law passed by democratically elected representatives, and you five have used this narrow question – Is *Hillary: The Movie* electioneering? – as an excuse to rewrite the law to your liking. There's a phrase for this. You know it well. You used it a lot in your confirmation hearing.

(**ROBERTS** *nods.*)

Judicial activism. You said you reject judicial activism, and you would lead with *judicial restraint*. You said Justices are referees, not players, in American jurisprudence.

ROBERTS. I did.

SOUTER. And yet, today, you, Anthony Kennedy, Samuel Alito, Antonin Scalia, and Clarence Thomas, five men, who were not voted in and cannot be voted out, you rewrote decades of Congressional law. In my opinion, money is not speech, and corporations are not people. And whatever the flaws of the American political system, a dearth of corporate money is not one of them. From an historical perspective, I think this decision will be looked upon as a moment of shame for the Supreme Court. A point of dishonor and embarrassment. Your court, Mr. Chief Justice.

Those are the highlights of my dissent.

(**SOUTER** *leaves Roberts' office.*)

THE FUTURE. The public finds out how the Court ruled on a case when the Chief Justice stands and announces the decision from the bench. Roberts didn't announce Citizens United until the last day before their summer recess.

ROBERTS. Case number 08-205, *Citizens United versus The Federal Election Commission*, is set for *re*-argument –

BOSSIE. Re-argument! What the...

ROBERTS. After the summer recess, on September 9. And this time, consider as the questions presented to the Court –

BOSSIE. He tells us to argue it differently! The Chief Justice tells us to challenge the constitutionality of BCRA! He's like, don't say you're complying with BCRA, tell us the law is wrong! And we were like, okay! Will do! See ya in September!

THE FUTURE. But that wasn't the last order of business that day, was it.

ROBERTS. And now we note, with sadness, that this is the last session in which our friend and colleague Justice David Souter will be on the bench with us. We wish him the best in his well-deserved retirement.

HOPE OF. He retired 'cause of this, right? Citizens United broke Souter.

THE FUTURE. I mean, we don't *know* that.

HOPE OF. He was done. A lot of people were. This decision made cynics out of a lot of people who loved and respected the highest court in the United States.

THE FUTURE. And since Roberts set the case for re-arguing, we can't read Souter's original dissent. It's no longer part of the public record. By rescheduling, the John Roberts Court saved face.

HOPE OF. But David Souter is a class act. He was very gracious on his last day.

SOUTER. Dear Colleagues, I will try to leave you with some sense of what our common service has meant to me. This Court accounts for the finest moments in my life, as we have agreed or argued over those things that matter to decent people in a civil society. For nineteen terms I have lived this life with you, all of us sharing our own best years with one another working side by side as fellow servants and as friends. I will not sit with you at our bench again after our Court rises for the summer this time but neither will I retire from our friendship which has held together despite the pull of the most passionate dissent. It has made the work lighter through all my tenure here and for as long as I live, I will be thankful for it. Yours affectionately, David.

(He leaves, and we shift to another day at the Supreme Court.)

THE FUTURE. September 9, 2009. The re-argument.

HOPE OF. We're gonna let the new Justice tell this part.

*(**SONIA SOTOMAYOR** takes center stage. During this, the rest of the cast set aside their costumes and sit at **SOTOMAYOR** and **GINSBERG**'s feet, like school kids.)*

SOTOMAYOR. Hola. Me llamo Sonia Sotomayor. I'm so proud to be the first Latinx Supreme Court Justice. Anyone here from the Boogie Down Bronx?

(To those who shout out.) Wepa!

(If no one is from the Bronx.) Well, please come visit, it's a beautiful part of the country.

(To the others onstage.) Fun fact: the *re*-argument of Citizens United was my first oral argument as a Supreme Court Justice.

EVERYONE ELSE. Welcome! Congrats! *(Etc.)*

SOTOMAYOR. Thank you. It didn't go how I wanted. Money won. Some would say Free Speech won but I say: money won. Because, well, money wins a lot. And because no matter how well the F.E.C. argued…

*(She gestures to the **FIVE JUSTICES** who voted in the majority.)*

KENNEDY. My mind was already made up.

THOMAS. So was mine.

ROBERTS. Me too.

ALITO. Samesies.

SCALIA. Same same same!

SOTOMAYOR. Section 203 of BCRA never stood a chance.

GINSBURG. Yet another depressing day to be Ruth Bader Ginsburg.

SCALIA. If it makes you feel any better, I die pretty soon. *(To the audience.)* A few months later, Antonin Scalia has a heart attack and dies.

> *(He has a heart attack and dies. They all regard his corpse on the ground...)*

SOTOMAYOR. Qué lástima...

THOMAS ACTOR. Can I take this off? I don't want to be Clarence Thomas anymore.

ALITO ACTOR. And I don't want to be Samuel Alito anymore.

ROBERTS ACTOR.	**KENNEDY ACTOR.**
Yeah, me either.	Honestly, I kinda hate this dude.

> *(**BREYER, SOTOMAYOR,** and **STEVENS** start taking off their robes. **SCALIA** stays dead on the floor a little longer. Maybe the others have to step over him. **GINSBURG** stays in her robe as she collects the robes the others take off.)*

BREYER ACTOR. In working on this play, I've become a big fan of Stephen Breyer, but I'm taking this off too. What's the point of wearing his robe if his vote doesn't even matter?

SOTOMAYOR ACTOR. I hear you. It sucks to always be on the losing side, one vote away.

> *(Here the **LIBERAL JUSTICES** could break into song about always being one vote away in the style of "One Call Away" by Charlie Puth.*)*

SCALIA ACTOR. *(Jumps up.)* Can I throw something out there?

HOPE OF. Please.

---

*A license to produce *Citizens United* does not include a performance license for any third-party or copyrighted music. Licensees should create an original composition or use music in the public domain. For further information, please see Music Use Note on page 3.

*(Re: **SCALIA** jumping up from the dead.)* Hi.

SCALIA ACTOR. Hi. Man, playing dead makes you really appreciate what a gift life is.

(Clearing his throat, to the audience.) David Bossie took a break from running Citizens United to run Donald Trump's presidential campaign.

EVERYONE ELSE. Man. No kidding. Oh jeeze. There you go. *(Etc.)*

SCALIA ACTOR. And back in 1988? *He* was the guy who came up with the Willie Horton ad campaign.

THOMAS ACTOR. Wait, you mean those racist TV ads that sunk Dukakis and got George Bush the First elected?

SCALIA ACTOR. Yup. David Bossie has been in the business of manipulating public ignorance to put *his* guys in office for *decades*. *This* is the man whose lawsuit rewrote the nation's campaign finance laws.

THE FUTURE. Dang.

SCALIA ACTOR. So I guess my question is: is free speech really all that?

HOPE OF. Whoa.

THE FUTURE. That question is kinda blowing my mind.

HOPE OF. Totally. Free speech feels *so core* to our values, it never occurred to me to question it.

KENNEDY ACTOR. Well, because we learn that regulating and punishing speech is what dictators do.

SCALIA ACTOR. Sure. And I *don't* want to live in a dictatorship. But there has to be a middle ground between a repressive dictatorship and letting any old greedy, racist millionaire buy up our media channels to say whatever the fuck he wants, right?

THE FUTURE. Uhhh –

SCALIA ACTOR. Whatever the heck he wants, right?

HOPE OF. Maybe free speech is like lots of good things: basically good – *but* – it gets messed up if you take it too far.

SOTOMAYOR. As the president who appointed me said, "Extremists are always wrong."

HOPE OF. Wait, who appointed you again?

SOTOMAYOR. President Barack Hussein Obama.

HOPE OF. I knew that. I just love hearing his name.

> (**GINSBURG** *walks among the students, collecting their robes.*)

GINSBURG. The case *Citizens United* made a lot of people bitter. It made us feel like giving up.

BREYER ACTOR. Even you?

GINSBURG. Even me. But you know what I remember, when I feel cynical?

KENNEDY ACTOR. What?

GINSBURG. I spent most of my life on *that* side of the bench. The fight for gender equality started on your side. The Court didn't *give* women rights, we demanded them!

SOTOMAYOR ACTOR. *(To the audience.)* That's true of every right you've ever heard of. They weren't given to us by the Court, they were demanded by the fourth branch of government: Us.

EVERYONE. The People.

ALITO ACTOR. And those battles were lost many many times before they were won.

THOMAS ACTOR. You can say that again.

ALITO ACTOR. Those battles were lost many many times before they were won.

GINSBURG. Don't give up, don't be cynical, get to work! Get out there, be the beautiful geniuses you are, in your regular clothes, with the powerful names you were given.

> (*At* **GINSBURG**'s *gesture, everyone onstage goes around and says their names.*)

And then, after you've done some time on that side of the bench, educating yourself –

SCALIA ACTOR. Writing letters –

ROBERTS ACTOR. Arguing –
ALITO ACTOR. Posting –
HOPE OF. Petitioning leaders –
THE FUTURE. Voting people in –
THOMAS ACTOR. Voting people out –
BREYER ACTOR. Organizing –
SOTOMAYOR ACTOR. Protesting –
STEVENS ACTOR. Supporting –
KENNEDY ACTOR. Dissenting –
SCALIA ACTOR. Volunteering for candidates –
ROBERTS ACTOR. Running for office –
GINSBURG. After all that, maybe you'll want to put these robes back on.

Because, you are the Hope Of The Future.

I can't wait for you to take us there.

End of Play

www.ingramcontent.com/pod-product-compliance
Lightning Source LLC
Chambersburg PA
CBHW072017290426
44109CB00018B/2264